In Memory of the Good Old Days

Robert Lot King

Edited By: My loving wife, Mary Francies King
Co-Editor: Mariah Leigh King

iUniverse, Inc.
Bloomington

In Memory of the Good Old Days

iUniverse books may be ordered through booksellers or by contacting:

iUniverse
1663 Liberty Drive
Bloomington, IN 47403
www.iuniverse.com
1-800-Authors (1-800-288-4677)

ISBN: 978-1-4620-1249-7 (pbk)
ISBN: 978-1-4620-1250-3 (cloth)
ISBN: 978-1-4620-1251-0 (ebk)

Printed in the United States of America

iUniverse rev. date: 4/21/2011

In Loving Memory of my Parents Paul and Daisy King

Contents

Introduction

My name is Robert Lot King. I was born in Southern Indiana on May 14, 1937. I grew up mostly in a rural area and small towns. I attended school in a one room setting with different grades in different rows and walked two miles to school. There were mud roads and lots of woods that us children loved to play in. There were no interstate highways, mostly dirt and gravel roads. Many folks traveled to town by horse and wagon to do their shopping. I attended bible school at Kentucky Mountain Bible Institute and completed a four year course of study for minister's, under the instruction of the Church of the Nazarene. I was ordained in the Church of The Nazarene and spent most of my life pastoring and preaching the gospel. During this time, I started a letter ministry, messages written out in manuscript style, that were sent to several states. This greatly helped me in my passion for the ministry and passion for writing.

This entire story is original and true about the living conditions in the early forties during World War Two after the great depression. It is toned to the good old days so often mentioned by our older generation. The precious memories of our older folks will take them back in time and they will smile as they read and remember the early years of their life. The younger generation will also enjoy this story as they learn of the history and draw insight of how their elders lived in those days gone by. All ages will benefit and enjoy this story as I reach back in time and rediscover living conditions that have mostly been forgotten. These days seem like only yesterday as I go back in memory.

Along with the Good Old Days my story also includes several other parts. Part Two is my journey of trials and victories through my preaching journey that started in the mountains of eastern Kentucky. This part contains many heartwarming experiences where the hand of God was revealed many times as I ministered over the years, giving vision of God's presence. Part Three consists of mine and my wife's ministry leaving the mountains and returning to Indiana. Also, there are several messages on faith and hope included in this section.

Section Four is committed to creation and how it all happened. Here you will find common sense proof of a living God explained in detail. All who read this account will agree that there is a living God without question. Creation will take on a new dimension in your faith in God that will erase negative questions about His eternal existence and who made it all. The words in this section will keep your attention because every word is true. All spiritual statements are backed by the authority of God's word which brings truth and fact to its highest level that can be attained. In this age of unbelief growing at an alarming rate, the time has come for believers to hold hands and form a chain of faith that Satan cannot break. This fourth part is explicitly directed to build faith in the one and only living God who made the Heavens and the Earth. Read part four carefully with your God given common sense and understanding. The evidence given is without question proof of the existence of a master mind with unlimited abilities that can only be the all wise God, who made all things well. Part Five is the concluding chapters with inspirational messages on our Christian faith.

PART ONE

IN MEMORY
OF THE
GOOD OLD DAYS

CHAPTER ONE
The Good Old Days

HAVING LIVED THESE DAYS myself beginning in 1937, my story is an original journey that started during a time I call the good old days and goes back in time to relive from memory how it was. The good old days of long ago have vanished along with the changing times. However, I grew up in the early forties which gave me much insight to those times that I wish to share in this book.

I remember the long wail of the steam engines chugging across the country valley as its whistle pierced the stillness of the night. It was the loneliest sound I can ever remember. The crowing of a rooster at sunrise, while sitting on the gate by the barn seemed to wake up nature all at once. An occasional Model-A Ford chugging by on the gravel road as the rocks rattle off the fenders, bring back the sounds of the past to my memory's ear. The squeaking chains of our porch swing on a warm summer evening told me of mother and dad resting from a long days work as they read the evening paper and shared the news. In the early morning hours the sudden blast of a shotgun echoing through the woods told of our Dad hunting squirrels for the meat that we so often had for our meals. Mother would cook biscuits and gravy with fried squirrel, fried potatoes and green beans from our garden. Warm homemade bread, topped off with fresh homemade butter and blackberry jelly with fresh milk from our own cows was quite a tasty meal. One of my daily chores was gathering eggs from our chicken house, and sometimes I would discover a chicken snake in the nest with lumps in its body from swallowing our eggs.

In the good old days the world was moving at a much slower pace with limited technology. The top speed of an automobile was about forty or fifty miles per hour, that is if you owned a Model -A Ford. The farmers shucked corn by hand and plowed their fields with a team of horses or mules. This made the plowing, disking and planting a very slow process. Today we have powerful four wheel drive tractors, with tires I can barely reach the top of, that can pull twelve row corn planters. Today's farmers ride in an enclosed air-conditioned cab with a radio and power steering that you can guide with one finger.

The good old days called for much labor and dedication to work; most everyone had the responsibility of chores and a job to do. At the end of a hard day's work there was no television to watch, and many didn't even have a radio to listen too. Those who did had a simple battery radio for lack of electricity. The programs, such as Popeye and Olive or the Lone Ranger and Tonto, were quite exciting to us children. When the masked Lone Ranger riding the great white horse cried out "Hi-O-Silver Away," I would get goose bumps, it would seem so real. The sound effects were so realistic I could actually see the actors in my mind.

In the good old days Mom would wash our clothes on a wash board with homemade lye soap in a tub of water, and then wring the water out of them by hand. After that she would hang them on a wire clothes line that stretched across the yard, and pin them to the line with clothes pins. I can still see the white sheets waving in the wind and warm sunlight as they dried. Coal stoves placed in two or three rooms in our house were common for our heat in the cold winters. Another one of my daily chores was to dump the stoves' ashes on our driveway and fill all the coal buckets. The work was hard and the days were long, but since responsibility was instilled into us children at a very young age, we did our chores without too much complaint or gripe.

Sunday was a day of rest and always a day we all looked forward to. Mother would always fix something special for Sunday dinner such as fried chicken or chicken and dumplings. Once in a while she would fix a beef roast with homemade noodles with a cake or pie, and sometimes homemade lemonade. Sunday was a very special day in our home and we always went to church to worship God.

The fall was always a fun time and the moods were very high. Harvest time on the farm meant good times as the pantry and cellar were filled with many good things to eat. Grain and cattle were taken to the market and sold, and for a while most had a few dollars in the bank or in a fruit jar. Also, in the fall, families would get together with buckets and bags and would search through the woods for hazelnuts, hickory nuts and walnuts. The nuts required some drying out and by Christmas time they were tasty and ready for a Christmas treat. Homemade candy such as divinity, taffy and fudge with fresh nuts mixed in was the best candy I've eaten. The good old days is a good description for those days of my past in many ways, and though times were hard, the days were still filled with many positive things that bring within me a longing for the missing past. I wrote a song about those Good Old Days:

Oh how I long to see it once more, that old
country home by the maple tree grove.
A faded white house and a tattered old barn, memories
of Mother, Dad, the family and me
Seems I can see that old country road, with dust on
the mail box, and the sunsets of gold.
With a rusty old fence by the June apple tree, where
dad raised a garden, for the family and me.

When I remember these days I remember all the good, positive events and conditions that bring joy to my memory. If I were to dwell only on the hard trials, labors and struggles or all the primitive living conditions, how we went without the many things we have today, my memory would be clouded with negative thoughts. However, when I reflect back to the good old days, I remember the sweet taste of the positive events that brought joy into my life. We from those days have a longing to relive and revisit the old familiar path once walked that we call the good old days of yesterday, and taste the sweet memories that will never be forgotten. Don't think badly of those with white and gray hair who get a sparkle in their eyes when in conversation they tell you about the good old days gone by.

This is the story about life in the past, about courage and faith during a time in history that is called the good old days when times were hard and life was simple. Stored in the avenues of my mind are precious and sweet spiritual memories that I will treasure forever because those spiritual moments were the beginning roots of my salvation.

I was only a child of four years old when my parents were converted. At that time their lives were in shambles and filled with sin. It was in the final years of the Great Depression and World War Two was just beginning. Times were hard and money was scarce, and doing without many things was the everyday plan. Running to the store and buying a candy bar and a bottle of pop just didn't happen for us children because there was barely enough money to pay the house rent and buy a few groceries. Because of the war, gasoline and food such as sugar and flour were rationed and the government issued stamps according to the size of the family to buy these items. Many were in want and jobs just didn't exist, so people were struggling just to survive. The Great Depression brought with it the worst days America had ever faced, and it was right at the time of it that Mother and Dad were married. As this was the beginning of the war, many materials were hard to come by. I remember when a tire would get a break in it, Dad would take another old tire and cut a piece out of it for a boot to cover the break. A new tire just wasn't available or possible for our car. After the Depression most people tried to get their lives back together as jobs begin to pick up once again. The war was going full force and there were many factories that were making planes, bullets and other supplies to give to the soldiers. Mom was able to get a job helping make bullets for fifty cents an hour which was a great help for our family.

Before the war, our Dad was a drunkard and a gambler, and the money he would earn was wasted away with his bad habits. This took food away from our table and there was very little to eat. Mom would make water gravy and water biscuits because there was no milk in the house. My health was critical at age two. I could not walk and I became so weak Mom would tie a diaper around me in a chair to keep me sitting up. I had what they called pin worms so bad I was dying. I remember Mom would give me a teaspoon of turpentine mixed with sugar as medicine, but it didn't work. Mom, many years later, told how my eyes were beginning to set with the look of death on my face. They finally took me to a doctor who gave me pills to rid my body of the pin worms. It worked and I soon began to walk and run like a normal little boy. All I needed was one trip to the doctor, and even then I believe the Lord had a hand in it. When God looks down on humanity He doesn't overlook a single person.

On a good day Dad would catch fish from the Patoka River near Huntingburg, Indiana, or he would hunt rabbits and squirrels for our meat. Mom would can lots of blackberries in the summer and I can remember many times when she poured blackberry juice over a slice of bread on our plate and that was all we had in the house to eat. However, with a little sugar sprinkled over it we liked it. I could never figure out when we would go to my uncle's house, why after everyone had already eaten, milk would still be left in their glasses and food in the bowls when at our house nothing was ever left over. I remember many times sneaking into his kitchen and drinking milk out of a glass that someone left, and reaching in the bowls with my bare hands eating their leftover food. No one ever knew about it but me, and I made more than one trip to my aunt's kitchen where I found food for myself as a hungry growing boy.

It was sin and the devil that led Dad to the beer taverns and the card tables where he spent our money that was so desperately needed for food. Of course, Dad was blinded by Satan and he didn't realize that at the time, but none the less that was the condition we were in when Jesus came by and turned our family on the road to prosperity and happiness. At the time of Mom and Dad's conversion, I was four years old and that is when these precious memories took root in my heart. Going to church was the happiest day of the week and we all couldn't wait for Sunday to come because where peace was given, peace was found. We found where the real earthly treasures were, and every time we went to church we found another nugget of gold to store in our treasure chest. I remember how Dad would talk about the Sunday message for days telling all who came to our house or in the homes we would visit. I learned very early that when Jesus really comes into a person's heart they want to tell everyone about the joy they have found in salvation. A silent heart is a heart in need because God gives overflowing grace, and it's a natural thing to have an ambition to tell others of the love of God you have received. What God has done for one, He will do for others. This should be our song sung every day, everywhere we go.

The day dad was saved the Church of the Nazarene in Huntingburg Indiana was in their fifth week of revival with Evangelist Roy Bettcher and song Evangelist Doug Slack. To advertize the services they attached a speaker to the top of their car and they would drive all over town inviting people to come out to the revival meeting. It worked very well. One of the Evangelists told me many years later that Mother went to the altar, and we four children went with her. I don't remember that, but I was at the altar for my first time in my life as Mother repented and gave her heart to the Lord as she was gloriously saved. As soon as Mother was saved she and the church began to pray for her drunkard husband. I have learned when God's children begin to pray things begin to happen and God truly answers their prayers.

During the fifth week of the revival, Dad was on his way to church, but his plan wasn't to attend but to drag Mom out of the service. He left the tavern drunk and made his way to the church with his drinking buddies tagging along behind to watch the fun, but God had other plans. Dad was six feet four inches tall and very thin. He had steel caps on the toes of his shoes and steel plates on the bottoms. As he made his way down the sidewalk, stepping high as a drunk does, it must have been a noisy sight as he clicked down the walk to the church. As he entered the door of the church the power of God took over and Dad went to the altar, sat flat down on the floor with his legs crossed, and said: "I want to get saved." God gloriously saved my dad that night in 1941 and he never looked back. The evangelist wrote a song and often sang it in meetings that went like this: "I went there to fight but I'll tell you that night something got hold of me, yes something got hold of me." Certainly something got hold of Dad that night that changed his life forever.

Dad went to be with Jesus just this past year at age ninety four. Everyone that ever knew him knew that something truly got hold of him and placed his feet upon the solid rock where he staked his claim forever. This is where my spiritual roots began as Dad and Mother took us to church every Sunday morning, Sunday night, and Wednesday prayer meeting. Church was never optional in our home. When company came to spend the weekend, Mom would tell them, "Today is Sunday and we go to church." I can still see her bravely standing there and looking them right in the eye as she said, "We are going to church I hope you will go with us, but if not we'll see you when we get home." Nothing took the place of church ever.

Dad would take us to every revival meeting that was in reasonable distance of our home. I can still remember our old Model-A-Ford chugging along with the dust flying on that old gravel road with the six of us and most often our neighbor kids sitting on our laps. I can remember upon arriving at church the good Pastor would count our load as we would pile out of the car. It would please Dad and Mother, and the more they could stuff in our car the better they liked it. They were doing something for Jesus who had done so much for them which taught us children that anything we can do for God is a good thing. Christians should count it a joy to do something for God.

Many family members and friends found their way to salvation by witnessing Mom and Dad's. Some even went out into the world preaching the gospel. Mom and Dad found the joy of Jesus, and they worked their whole life inviting and hauling anyone who would go with them to church. They wanted everyone to find the peace and joy that they had found in Jesus.

When we would go to church at Huntingburg I was very shy, and when the children would go up front to sing I would hide behind the bigger boys so no one could see me. I was only four or five years old but I remember to this day a song our Pastor Rev. Small called his favorite that we would sing every Sunday. "*I know the lord will make a way for me, if I live a holy life shun the wrong and do the right, I know the lord will make a way for me.*" These are the memories that are dear to me and they will be forever sealed in my heart. I truly have learned the Lord has made a way for me, and he has made a way for all who will come to Him.

Today I am retired from my pastoring career of the past 35 years, but the flame still burns as I write this book and recall the many memories in the Lord. When I was first called to preach I was called to Petersburg, Indiana for supply preaching, and something very special happened. In my message I told how I used to sing that little song by the often request from Pastor Small, "*I know the Lord will make a way for me.*" After the service a lady was leading a blind man to the front who wanted to introduce his self to me, it was Brother Small who had long ago been my pastor as a four year old boy. It was a great blessing for me, and it must have been a great blessing for him. God has a way of giving unexpected blessings to His children as we follow His will.

After Mother and Dad were saved, they were to be baptized. Dad said if there was more to get he wanted it all. I remember his testimony, I had heard many times, "I was saved on Friday, sanctified on Saturday, and baptized on

Sunday. I got three works of God's grace in one weekend." So we arrived at the Patoka River, near Huntingburg Indiana, for the baptizing service. The water was a little swift and when they baptized Mother she lost her footing and was carried down the river. Mom could not swim a lick but she could float on her back, and float she did! Two young men who were good swimmers swam out and brought Mother back to safety. I suppose no one will ever forget the day they baptized Mother as the church congregation stood on the banks of the muddy Patoka River and sang *Shall We Gather at the River*. Mom was rescued that day not only from the swift waters of the river, but also from the world of sin that was drowning her family and destroying her home. Jesus truly is the master of the raging rivers of life, and when He says, "Peace, be still," there will be a great calm.

Those years seem like yesterday and sometimes it surprises me of all the things I can remember. To relive the past is an experience that I have never done before in this fashion and I am getting a blessing as I recall my life as a child and my growing up years.

Many homes in those days were without electricity so everyone had ice boxes where they kept their food from spoiling. There was an ice man just like the mailman who delivered ice door to door on a truck with a canvas thrown over his load of big blocks of ice. Those who ordered ice had a card which had the amount of pounds they wished to buy on it. The card had different amounts on each side such as twenty, twenty five or maybe even fifty pounds. The customer would place the card in the window of their home with the amount they wanted turned up. The ice man would use a pick and chip just the right amount off the large block of ice in one single square. Then he would grab it with a special made pair of ice hooks and carry it into their kitchen and place it in their ice box. I remember many times children would gather around while he was chipping the ice in hopes a chip would fall their way and they would scramble to get it. A piece of ice was a treat if you were lucky enough to get one. Sometimes the kind man would chip off a piece for each child that was there, maybe to keep us from chasing the truck down the street. I can still taste that chip of ice melting in my mouth on a hot summer day it was as good as a modern day Popsicle to us children.

I remember my Uncle Joy who had his own invention to keep food fresh in the wintertime. He built a frame with screen wire over it and he mounted it to the outside of his window so all he had to do was raise the window and place their butter, milk, and meats in the box. It worked fine in the winter months when it wasn't too cold. Everyone did what they had to do to meet the needs of the times. One winter I stayed with my grandparents for a few days and my bed was made of straw, and very noisy. It was made by taking two sheets, sewing them together, and stuffing the pouch full of straw. Sometimes the sharp ends of the straw would stick me, but it made a cheap mattress. I remember being sent to the garden to get potatoes for supper where a large mound was hollowed out and filled with straw. There was a hole with a piece of burlap over it where you could reach your arm inside and get the potatoes out. This not only protected them from freezing but they stayed fresh all winter and into the spring. The good old days had its hard places but it also had its blessings.

Our lives were changed from day one after Mother and Dad were converted. Everything in life seemed to fit together in a harmony that we had never known before. Our lives became filled with meaning and a purpose. We were now a part of the family of God where people cared for one another and shared each others' burdens. I still remember how powerful the preachers would preach and my young heart would get under conviction. Many times I would go to the basement during the alter call and people would go to the altar almost every service.

World War Two was going strong and people were hurting from loss of sons and husbands. Their hearts were broken and heavy with pain and they found help in the church where people could pray the glory down. The churches were full in those days as people come flooding in, and many were giving their hearts to the Lord. I have learned that the only real peace is in the Lord. I saw as a child the hurt and tears of a weeping mother and dad who had lost their precious son who was killed in action. Every Sunday we would hear of more in our community who were killed or missing in action. Many nights we would have blackouts which meant all lights would be out in the country as well as in the town. It was always scary for us children as we sat around in the house in the dark with all the lights in the neighborhood out.

I can remember hearing hundreds of planes flying over very low, carrying troops and supplies to the military bases all over America, preparing to go to the battle fronts. I remember the comic books filled with battle scenes and our American planes would always shoot the enemy down in a trail of smoke. Of course the artist would always make us the winners in battle. I've always believed that war has no winners but only tears, broken hearts and destruction, no matter what nation is involved.

One day when I was about nine years old, Mother and Dad went to town to shop and we children were left at home to play. Suddenly cars started passing by, blowing their horns without ceasing. About that same time Mom and Dad and another car started up our long driveway and they too were blowing their horns. We knew that something had happened and it had, the war was finally over. It was the happiest time I can ever remember as people were celebrating all over the nation. I knew that now the clouds of smoke and the sound of exploding bombs would be silenced around the world. Now nations could rebuild many cities that lay in ruins and people could walk the city streets without fear and trembling. Our soldiers could return home to their families and rebuild their lives once again.

These are the days of my childhood that remain in my memory and give me an appreciation for the simple things of life that so many take for granted in this age we live. All of these events that I witnessed truly affected my life, and especially my spiritual life. I learned early the difference a Christian life can make in a family, and I have seen the horrible results of families that left God out of their lives. I watched their families fall apart as sin ruled in all their actions and their children ended up in foster homes as sin led to divorce and separation. Sin has no happy endings, but God has a plan that always ends with a happy ending in Heaven, where peace will rule forever in a city of unending joy where men never die. I grew up in church and was taught at a very young age about sin, Heaven, and Hell. Mother and Dad taught us children right from wrong straight from the pages of the word of God.

One night when I was only seven we had just gotten home from a revival meeting and I had gone to bed in a small room downstairs. I was crying when Mother came into my room and wanted to know why I was crying. I told her I was going to be a preacher. However that night was soon forgotten and little did I know that many years later I would answer God's call to preach His blessed gospel. As I look back in time, I'm assured that the good old days hold treasures that make the trials and struggles of life seem like nothing today, and the trials of faith that we endured is the very fuel in our hearts that wins the battles that so often come. I believe rough roads make strong runners for Jesus and He knows just how to condition us for the road ahead. The following pages in this book will reveal the work and journey of a preacher and pastor for Jesus Christ and the many memories that I hold dear to my heart. Also in these next pages are the living conditions we faced without electricity or running water in the early forties. Can you believe there was no television to watch?

Sometimes in the rush and stress of life, when surrounding circumstances crowd around me and I need an escape from the bondages of everyday life, I find comfort and peace by revisiting the past. I enjoy going back, even to my boyhood days and glean, from my past those good and precious memories of Mother, Dad, the family and me. In my way of thinking my memory holds treasures that make the heart glad. I envision a small red haired boy wearing bib overalls running barefoot among the maple trees that surrounded our country home. Life was such an adventure for me and my blue eyes were wide, drinking in all of God's beautiful creation.

Every day was like a new adventure for me, and I wondered what exciting event would each day hold. My expectancy for the new day was high, as the morning sunlight would break through with golden streamers of light shining through the maple trees in our yard. At the same time, birds of many varieties would pierce the silence with sweet music. I've often thought, not only does God drive back the darkness of the night, but He sends the song birds to sing to us to send cheer along with the sunshine of each morning. God has given us all the elements in life for our complete happiness and joy.

I can still see those chubby little hands of Mother's as she would peel potatoes for supper. It was like a work of art, she could peel a potato in the blink of an eye. Her loving hands were always working to make life better for her family. When we all gathered around the table no one dared to eat until Mom or Dad would thank God for the food that He gave to us. It's been many years since I sat at Mother's table, but even now I lick my lips in memory of those wonderful meals she could prepare out of such simple things. Everything was made from scratch, the bread, the cake, everything was homemade. Food is ok today in our modern world, but somehow they have taken that special flavor out.

I remember Dad as well. I'll never forget his tall and handsome frame as he would tell his stories to others. He had a way of telling those stories that would keep us children spellbound while he told of his day at work. He would tell of his hunting experience on return from one that it was as if we walked through the woods by his side. Dad had a way of getting your attention and keeping it. With his dramatized stories, hand gestures and facial expressions he walked back and forth in the middle of the room. On Mother and Dad's anniversary he would always sing to Mother songs out of the twenties, one song I remember was called *That Sweet Gal of Mine.* I can still see the sweet smile on Mothers face while he sang to her.

We didn't have much as children, so it didn't take much to please us or make us happy. Most of our toys were homemade. Dad would take an old sock and stuff it full with other old socks and sew it tightly together. Then he would take an old, worn out broom and saw the handle just the right length for a bat, and we would play for hours. We called it rag ball. Dad would also take an old license plate, bend the corners back, and nail it to a stick of wood. Then he would get an old barrel hoop, and we would push it all over our property until we were out of breath. Also, Dad would take an old judge coffee can, cut the bottom out and nail it to the side of the barn. We children would take that old rag ball and toss it through the can for hours, this was our basketball. Our homemade toys gave us much pleasure and as I look back I see the love and care Mom and Dad gave to us children that made our life better. It may not have been a real ball, but we had real fun.

In the evenings we would all sit in a circle in the living room and play a game we called, "Riddly, Riddly, Ree, I see something you don't see." Then the one who got the answer first would give the clues for the next game. Checkers was another favorite game that we often shared in the evenings. We also played a game called hide the thimble. We would cover our eyes while someone hid Mom's sewing thimble, and the one who found it got to hide it next.

We had no T. V. or electricity so we used oil lamps for light; we made do with what we had. Mom would pop a pan of corn to add a treat to our evening of games. We seldom had a bottle of pop to go with the corn, and when we did, Mom would divide one bottle with two or three of us. Having less makes you appreciate the little things in life. In our world of abundance today, the minds of our children are filled with too many wants.

I remember my two sisters would take a stick and scratch a bunch of squares in the yard where they could find bare dirt without grass. The girls would take a rock to mark their place in the squares where they hopped. They called their game Hop Scotch, and they played it for hours. Playing these outdoor games was common in those days because children didn't have all the trinkets to keep them indoors like they do now.

Summertime was always a very welcome time for all. Every year, on the first day of May, we were allowed to go barefoot, and for the rest of the summer we seldom wore shoes. Summer brought with it garden season and we always had a large garden. Mom would can lots of vegetables, fruits, and jellies to last us till the next summer. I don't remember ever going hungry after Dad's conversion, but I do remember good, home cooked meals when life was at its best during those good old days.

Since we had no electricity, storing food in the summer was a bit of a problem. We would take our milk and butter, put it in a bucket with a rope, and lower it down in our well to keep it cool and fresh. As stated earlier, Dad would hunt and trap rabbits and squirrels for our meat. We always had a cow to milk, and chickens to supply eggs. Sunday was always a special day as we went to church to worship God with our friends in Christ, and we would often share dinner with friends at their homes.

In the good old days there was a lot of manual labor with limited machinery and power tools. I remember how hard Dad had to work to provide for our family. During the war, he worked in a furniture factory for fifty cents an hour. He later got a job driving a coal truck which paid one dollar an hour, and many times he would have to shovel the entire load by hand. Dad would get home late after a ten hour day, but we would always wait till he got home before we would eat supper. I don't ever remember our dad complaining of the hard work. He left all us children memories that will never leave us.

Dad made friends with everyone and I never knew of him having an enemy. He was well liked by everyone who knew him after God put sweetness in and took the devil out. He had lots of friends and would often trade cars or guns with them. I remember once he traded a coon dog for a Model-A-Ford and we rode to church every Sunday in what we thought was a nice car. After the messages on Sunday morning and night, Dad discussed them to everyone he talked to for the whole week. His witness and love of God and his church was known by all. We didn't know it then, but those were the best days of our lives as Mom and Dad taught us about God as we lived in the good old days of America.

When I think back in memory of Mother, Dad and the family, precious memories resurface. To me these are treasures of great worth. When I was seven years old, dad drove a coal truck and hauled coal to power plants and other companies. He also hauled lime for the farmers. I loved to go with Dad and ride in that big red truck. One of the farmers where he hauled lime had a big whiteface bull that roamed in the field where dad delivered the lime. The red truck made the bull very angry and sometimes the bull would charge toward the truck. One day, the large bull butted into the side of the truck where I was sitting. I've never forgotten how frightened I was as I heard the thud of his great head that shook the truck. It was quite an adventure to ride with Dad in that truck and I always hoped for another adventure every trip.

One day I asked dad if I could go with him on his route and thought he had said no. I went out in the garage crying and saying as many cuss words as I could think of over and over again. While I was having my cussing fit, I heard a horn blowing about two blocks away on the main highway. I ran outside the garage and saw it was Dad blowing the horn for me. I had misunderstood him, and he had meant for me to meet him on his way back through. However, as the truck pulled away, I realized my cussing fit had cost me that trip with dad. I don't ever remember having another one with such energy. I'll never forget that empty feeling as the big red truck pulled away and left me standing in my tears. I always thought it was my punishment from the Lord for doing something that I knew was very wrong.

I never heard cuss words in our home because my parents were Christians who lived by Gods rules. If we children used a cuss word, however small it may have been, a painful switch was always handy on top of Mother's cabinet. Cussing was never allowed in our home and that value was strictly enforced. I believe that today the words we use reveal the condition of our soul and where we stand with God. If we could imagine standing in the presence of Jesus, we would be very selective in the words we use. The fact is, we are standing in His presence wherever we go and He hears every word we speak. We should conduct our lives every day as if we are truly standing in God's presence.

One day on a trip in the truck, Dad and I crossed the Mt. Carmel Bridge. The water was at a flood stage and it was flowing over the road. Suddenly,

14

Dad stopped the truck and ran through the water and grabbed up a large fish that was wiggling its way across the road. Needless to say, we had fish for supper that night. That vision of Dad running through the water chasing that big fish will never be forgotten in my memory. Every trip with Dad held an adventure for this, at the time, small boy who was drinking in all of life's exciting events. For me, not getting to go with Dad in the truck was the worst thing that could happen.

Having Christian parents was a treasure of great worth for us children as we grew up. Today, as a minister of Jesus Christ, I realize more and more what a great difference it made in my life to have Godly parents who taught us right from wrong. They would never bend rules to fit our excuses when we did wrong. Mother and Dad's influence will walk with me all the way to eternity where we will meet once again forever, never to be separated ever again. Let us continue life at home with Mom and Dad.

One day Dad bought a big, red, milk cow that had very long horns. The man and woman who owned her were deaf and they could not speak. The cow was not used to voices and she would get wild at the sound of them. I would be milking her when someone would come into the barn and yell for me causing her to jump around and kick the bucket over. I was afraid of her and was glad when Dad decided to send her to the market. I'll never forget that day the men came with their truck to haul her to the market. Their truck had wooden racks on it, and when they got her in it, she leaped right through the wooden racks busting the whole side support into splinters. She ran to our fence and leaped over it with Dad right behind her. They both jumped the fence and Dad ran to her, took her by the horns, and threw her to the ground. Needless to say, they finally got her back into the truck, tied her down and away to the market she went.

We all looked to our Dad with great respect. We felt there was no one like him. Mother and we children would all wait anxiously for that old Model -A-Ford to roll into our driveway every day after work. He was our dad and we all loved him very much, and were so happy to see him. His love of God was revealed by his faithfulness to keep us children in church. Dad later got a job at International Harvester in Evansville, Indiana where he worked for many years. On his lunch break at work a small group would have a bible study which led to reaching others who were sinners. Several times Dad was instrumental in leading men to Christ and praying with them on the job. His boss warned them that they were going to have to stop during company time, but I don't think they ever did. Where is our passion for the lost today? I remember those days like they were yesterday and I find joy in going back in memory and reliving those precious moments of the good old days.

When I was in the first grade, we moved into a log house near Birdseye,

Indiana. My sister and I had to walk two miles to a little, red-roofed, one room school. The winters were cold and walking to school was hard. On the way there, my sister and I stuck our hands in both ends of the muff she wore around her neck, to keep our hands from freezing. At school, different grades would sit in different rows. At recess we would play in the woods that joined the school property and swing on the grape vines. We would also play tag.

During the winter, a cow pond near the school would freeze over and all the children would slide on the ice. One day I fell through the ice and got soaking wet! The bigger boys stripped me down, wrung out my long underwear in an outdoor toilet, then hung them on the fence to dry while I waited in the outdoor toilet freezing and shivering. My teacher heard of what happened, and she drove me home in her car to get dry clothes. I still shiver a little when I think of that day.

Our house in Birdseye had a long, dirt road for our driveway, and in rainy months, ruts were made by the skinny tires of the Model-A Ford. To make it up the drive to our house was a tricky task that involved staying in the ruts and giving the truck lots of gas to gun up the road. Many times that wasn't the case and our neighbors would come with their team of horses and pull us out of the mud.

About one hundred yards from the house in the woods there was a spring that never went dry, and we would carry our water to and from that spring in buckets during the winter and summer. Near the spring was a solid rock wall about ten feet high which made a perfect sliding board. We would wear holes in our trousers as we would slide down the rock. It was slick as a button and our very favorite place to play. Each fall we would gather nuts from the many Hickory nut trees that surrounded our house that would last us all winter.

When I was in the second grade we moved to a house in Pike County, Indiana. The school was in a tiny village called Coe. It had a bell with a rope tied to it which our teacher would ring to start class or to end recess. There was a hand pump in a well at the corner of the school with a tin cup for all to use. These were my first two years in school, and this is how it was in those days in 1943 and 1944.

The house we moved to had a striper pit a short distance from it. The pit was over a mile long and full of fish. I would stand on the bank and watch the fish swim by for hours. The pit became my most prized playground, and I would spend much time there every day. I made me a fishing pole out of one of Dad's bean poles, and Mom gave me string from meat packages from the store. I had no fish hooks so I would take a safety pin and bend it in the shape of a hook. I caught a few little blue gills but most of them would fall off because the thin pin could not hold them. Finally, Dad gave me a penny to buy a real fishing hook. I took my penny to a grocery store near the school and the kind man at the store gave me three fish hooks for my penny. I could hardly wait to get home that evening to try out my real fish hooks. I caught lots of fish and it made me very happy.

There was a willow tree that grew straight out of the bank of the pit. It lay on top of the water, and was large enough for me to lie down on. Underneath the tree was a nest where the rock bass would lay their eggs. I could reach in their nest with my hand while lying on the log, wiggle my finger to attract the attention of fish, and they would grab my finger. I would then quickly close my thumb on their mouth and catch them. It was my own little boy creation and it really worked, but no one believed my story. I had a path from the house all the way to that old pit and I don't believe a blade of grass grew as my bare feet often ran back and forth to fish in the pit.

When we first moved into the house, the people who moved out had left a goat. We children were small and we rode the goat like a pony every day. We didn't have much, but we had lots of fun and we were happy.

Visiting relatives was often an adventure as some of our relatives lived way out in the country. We sometimes would drive out to visit my dad's uncle Frank, who had no electricity and lived in a one room house. The bed and kitchen table were all in the same room. The most amazing thing about Uncle Frank was that he would catch opossums and tie them to their bed post. He'd keep them alive, and by doing this, they could have fresh meat when they wanted it. Keeping the opossums alive served as a way to keep the meat from spoiling since they had no refrigeration.

The old house that we lived in was heated by coal stoves. Dad would bank the stoves at night with ashes and by morning there was hardly any heat left at all. To bank with ashes was simply to take the ashes and pile them on top of the red coals. Many times I would cover my head up at night to keep out the cold, and when the winter winds whistled, we just snuggled up tighter in our bed. I believe those cold nights and the rugged life that we grew up by only conditioned us children to face the hard places ahead that were sure to come.

As we said earlier on Sunday we went to church, and church was never optional. When Sunday morning came Mother made sure we were ready. On Saturday evening Mom would polish four pairs of shoes and set them on the table to dry. Mom always prepared our clothes and had everything laid out on Saturday night so we could be at church on time. The Bible says where your heart is there will be your treasure also. Church was Mother and Dad's treasure that they had found, and we children had no excuse to not be just as faithful as we left home and started our own families.

As we grew up, we all knew how much God and church meant to our parents. When the oil lamps were blown out, and we were all tucked in our beds at night, the silence would be broken by Mother as she prayed out loud. I can remember lying there in my bed and listening to her words. Mom and Dad had brothers and family who were in the service during World War Two and were right in the heat of battle. As Mother prayed she would mention them, each one by name, and ask God to watch over them. I always believed He did. There was a certain plea in her voice that I just knew God was listening and that He would watch over our loved ones and bring them home safely. It didn't surprise us when every one of them actually did make it home safely.

News came that Mom's brother Bobby was operating a dozer when he hit a land mine on the side of a mountain. The dozer went over the side, but Bobby stayed safe and uninjured. I just knew it was because God was there as a result of Mother's prayer, and He sent his guardian Angels to look after a soldier who was fighting for our peace and safety. I have learned over the years that God can go where we can't go, and He can reach where we can't reach. In my desperations and impossible situations, I've learned to call on God to intervene.

Our family also learned that Dad's sister, Irene, and her family were picked up by the Japanese while visiting family in the Philippines. They were thrown into a prison camp where they spent three years. Mother prayed for their safety every night, so it didn't surprise us when our American paratroopers landed in the middle of their prison camp and rescued all that were left alive. It was a happy day when Aunt Irene, her husband, and three children walked in the door at my grandparent's home safe. We had a feast that day that would be hard to repeat. Anyone who knows the history of prison camps in World War Two would agree that it was a miracle that they were rescued, and I know it was God's miracle. His Guardian Angels took charge and rescued many that surely would have died from the many bombs that fell throughout the area.

When I revisit the good old days gone by, my greatest joy is to view the very hard places and struggles that God brought my family through. I believe God has a host of Angels that He often sends to spare His children from hurt and harm. There was a sparkle in Mother's eyes when she knew her God had answered her prayers. Faith in God will take you down a path of peace and trust as you journey through this uncertain world of evil intrusions from evil men that prey on the innocent with their demon led desires. Mother and Dad instilled into us children a true faith in the living God by their steadfast example of faith. They are both in Heaven today but their faith remains in our hearts. Today I am seventy three years old and I have preached the gospel of Jesus for thirty five years. The seed that Mother and Dad left behind is still bearing fruit for God's kingdom on Earth. It only reminds us of the results of planting the good seed of God's Holy word in the hearts of our children as they grow up. The good seed is a treasure of measureless worth. It is an eternal seed that will never die because it was given by the almighty God who is eternal forever.

My prayer and desire is that others will find faith in God in the same measure that I have, and that my stories will teach others the treasures of gleaning the good memories of the past and put aside the bad and hurtful ones. I have learned that my memory can be my worst enemy or it can be my best friend. Why should we beat ourselves up each night, lying in bed with all the bad memories, when we have good memories to gather from our lives that bring peace and rest? As Paul said, "Whatsoever things are good, whatsoever things are pure, think on these."

As I continue going back in memory it seems like only yesterday that we were young and full of energy. In those years our center point was fun and friends. It was then that our eyes looked into the world and all it had to offer us. Having fun would take our minds away from daily chores and trials. I remember all the hard work. We shucked corn by hand and the rows would seem to have no end. We would mow our yard with a push mower since there were no gas engines available. If you neglected to mow on time the grass would get high and it was very hard to mow. Neglect never did make life easier, but only brought with it hard work and bad results.

Everything we did had a system to go by. When we would milk the cow, Mom would strain it into a crock or large bowl and leave it to set over night. Then she would skim the heavy cream off the top the next day and save it until she had enough to make butter. Before we got a churn, Mom had to make butter by pouring the heavy cream into a gallon bucket and shake it until it would turn to butter. This took a lot of shaking. After the butter was formed and was taken out of the bucket, the remaining cream was butter milk, which we could drink. When bath time came Mom would heat the water on the wood stove and poor it into a galvanized wash tub, either in the kitchen or the back yard. Sometimes the water wasn't warm at all and we would be shivering by the time our bath was over.

In the evening we children would play in the yard and when Mother would call to us at supper time we wasted no time getting to the table. I don't ever remember anyone saying they didn't like what she prepared because Mom had a way of making the simplest things very tasteful. When we went to school Mom would give us a quarter for our dinner. With that I could buy a hamburger for a dime, a coke for a nickel, and a bag of chips for a nickel. That left a nickel for a candy bar. Unlike today, it didn't take much to please us and just a nickel ice cream cone or a bottle of pop was a great treat. Those days were happy moments for us children at home with Mom and Dad. We didn't need to look for greener grass, for the grass was greenest at home. Too many search in vain for greener grass when if we would look closely it's nearer than we realize.

I loved to go squirrel hunting with Dad, but I soon learned I had to be very quite. I never could figure out how Dad, who was six feet four inches tall, weighed two hundred pounds and wore number fourteen shoes, could slip through the woods so silently. I would try so hard, but try as I may a stick would snap and Dad would place his finger to his nose signaling me to be quite. One day Dad and I were walking in the edge of the woods and a rabbit jumped out in front of us. Dad quickly picked up a rock and threw it at the rabbit, which was running full speed. Amazingly, the rock hit the rabbit knocking it off its feet and our dog caught it. That night we had rabbit for supper. As I said earlier, life in those days as a small boy was exciting and every day was an adventure with Dad, as he often added dimension to adventure.

One day Dad bought several laying hens so we could have fresh eggs. The hens would run loose on the edge of the woods, and as they got older they would lay their eggs in a nest hidden in a briar patch. In the nest they would secretly hatch out baby chicks. Their wings were never clipped and they became very wild and lived in the trees in our woods. They could fly like quail sailing through the trees, and the only way we could have fried chicken to eat was for Dad to shoot them out of those trees.

As I go back in time to memory lane it refreshes my life and brings an inner smile to my heart. When I was young I thought we had so little compared to our rich neighbors, but today I realize we had riches beyond measure that no amount of money could buy. I had a home with Mother, Dad and the family. There are many things that I still remember like yesterday and they are memories that I wouldn't trade for any amount of money.

When I was young, I was afraid of the dark and if I forgot to close the chicken house door Mom would make me go close it. I would try to get out of it, but never did. In the dark I could see all kinds of shadows lurking in the yard as my imagination made it even worse. At night, I would lie in my bed and listen to the lonesome sound of the old steam engine passing through the countryside. The whistle was a long and lonely sound that would echo off into the night. It seemed as though every time Mom would hang the clothes on the line we would hear that whistle, and she would hurry to get her clothes in before the engine passed by our house. The long stream of black smoke shooting up out of the engine, and black particles from it would fall all over our yard and our clothes on the line. We would all help get the clothes in as quickly as possible so Mother wouldn't have to do her wash all over again.

In the night the only sounds you would hear were the distant barks of a neighbor's dog answering the barks of another dog. It was much different than this super age now where the roar of large trucks sound throughout the night without end. In the mornings I love to hear the call of crows because it has remained the same as it was many years ago, same as the whippoorwills in the evenings just before dark. In the early spring, millions of frogs' chirping would fill the atmosphere with the sure sound that spring was here and the long cold winter was over. At the first chirps I would hunt up my fishing pole and tackle box and head for my favorite fishing place, which was in the shallows of a lake where the water was warm and the fish were more active.

These and many other sounds in nature send us a true forecast of the coming seasons that even the Indians recognized. From the honking of the geese in the fall, that tell us to prepare for a long and cold winter, to the call of the Bob-White birds to their mates which tell us of new life that is about to begin. In the dry season I remember the dove calling for rain, and some really believed that it was a sure sign that rain was on the way. Distant thunder told us that a storm was on the way, and we would hurry to close the windows and doors. Many sounds in our world relate to an upcoming event, and many are a warning to prepare us, just like the biblical warnings that God sends to all humanity to be prepared for His coming.

My Teenage Years

As I grew into my teenage years, life became even more exciting and held many precious memories that I will never forget. When I was thirteen, we lived two miles down a gravel road and in the dry season you could write your name in the dust on the mailbox, which was about an inch thick from the passing automobiles. Our neighbors, the Thurman's, were within a rock's throw of our house. They had five sons that I would spend much time with visiting and playing. They had one of the first televisions that came out and all the neighborhood kids would fill their front room every Saturday and watch the Lone Ranger and his great white horse. It gave me goose bumps every time he would say, "Hi-O-SILVER-AWAY," and the great white horse would rear up as the masked man would wave good bye.

Our neighbors were farmers and raised lots of corn that they shucked all by hand. It was quite a scene to watch. Their mother would drive a small tractor that pulled a wagon which had a very high side board used as a backboard as the five sons and dad would shuck six rows at a time. They would pitch the ears of corn against the banking board and they would fall neatly into the wagon. It was amazing how quickly they could gather their harvest in the fall before winter would take hold. Mr. Thurman would place snakes in the corn crib to control the mice.

The Thurman's also raised four or five beef to butcher before winter and that was a highlight for us boys every year. Just before they would butcher them their dad would let us ride them. We would also hold on to their tails as they would drug us across the cow pasture while everyone would laugh and yell. Riding them was no easy task and soon we all would end up on the ground.

There were lots of woods nearby our house and in the fall we would go deep into them and hunt paw paws. We usually found several. There was an island surrounded by a creek full of paw paws, so we would wade across the creek, which came up to my chin, and fill our bags with paw paws. They tasted like bananas when they were good and ripe.

The road near our house was made with river gravel which was perfect for sling shots. I would gather a bucket full of just the right size rocks and practice every day. I became the best shot out of all of us kids. Charles Thurman was my age so we were good friends and did a lot of things together. We liked to go frog hunting, he would carry the bag and I would shoot them with my sling shot. The only way to get them was to shoot them just behind their head and if you hit them anywhere else they would leap into the water. I could do that most of the time but occasionally I would miss. Sometimes I would have someone throw a tin can into the air and once in a while I could even hit it with my sling shot.

One day when Charles and I were frog hunting we came upon a mine shaft that was filled with water. We decided if we dug our heels into the sloped bank we would be able to run across to the other side and we wouldn't have to walk all the way around. I made it just fine, but Charles slid down the bank into the deep water, and he didn't know how to swim. I'll never forget the fear that I saw on his face as he yelled, "Help me Bob I can't swim!" Immediately I leaped into the water and took hold of his arm and he hung on for dear life. There were cattails growing into the edge of the shaft and I was able to get hold of some and I pull us to safety. There must have been a guardian Angel present that day and God spared two young boys' lives. I haven't seen Charles for many years, but know he is retired out of the marines where he spent his career.

As for me, I spent most of my life preaching the gospel while pasturing several Churches. My teenage days were very special to me and they hold many precious memories that will always be with me. Life couldn't have been better for me down that gravel road, but soon bad news came. We were moving to town. I think I cried for a week as we loaded up and began moving. The hardest thing I ever faced in life was leaving my friends behind, which I had to do many times over the years since we moved numerous times. We used to say Dad moved every time the wind changed. I attended seven different schools during grade school, but in so doing I met many new friends that gave me many more memories to add to my life.

I soon reached the age of sixteen and I wanted to get a job, buy an automobile, find a girlfriend, fall in love, and get married. I soon found out that life doesn't work like that so quickly. I couldn't find me a job near home so I moved to the big city of Indianapolis where I put in several applications.

I remember walking many blocks to town where I would go to the picture show. One time I went they were showing a triple feature of Red Ryder, and Little Beaver. By the time it was over it was very late and I was a long way from home. I'll never forget that first night of my adventure walking home. As I looked up ahead of me I saw a tavern where several colored men were, most of them were drunk. I decided to cross the street so I wouldn't have to walk right through the middle of them, but they saw me and knew what I was doing. As I got across the street from them, they formed a line and begin marching behind me chanting, "hoop two three four, hoop two three four left, right, left, right." One of the men in the front had a broom on his shoulder. I was so frightened I ran the rest of the way home, and I could hear their laughter as I sped out of sight.

The next night I decided to take a new way home and it was late again. As I was walking home I came to a long flight of steps that led up the hill to another tavern. Just as I was in front of it I believe every window in the building broke out at the same time. There had been a riot break out and they were throwing pool balls. Once again I lay black marks with my sneakers as I sped off into the night.

I was beginning to dislike the big city and wish I was home under the safety of Mother and Dad. The days passed and I didn't find work so I returned home. I had been home just a few days when my cousin Dan came by and told me he had a job open for me in Evansville at a Pepsi Cola bottling Company. It was 1953 and I was sixteen years old and weighed one hundred and twenty seven pounds. My first day at work was hard. They were unloading a boxcar of sugar and as they dropped each one hundred pound bag of sugar onto my shoulder my knees buckled slightly. I figured if the other guys could do it so could I though, and I continued until we unloaded the entire load of bags.

My job in the plant was to stack the cases of drinks on a pallet as they came out of the machine, thirty cases on a pallet and three hundred and fifty cases an hour. It was glass bottles and wooden cases which weighed about fifty pounds each. I was hired in the busy season so they had me working twelve hours a day. I soon had blisters all over my hands and they became very sore, but I had made up my mind that I would never give up my job and become a loafer or lazy person. Work was hard for such a small boy but I soon got strong enough to hold my own as well as the others.

My pay was eighty cents an hour which amounted to six dollars and forty cents a day. After taxes I would take home twenty eight dollars a week.

I boarded with my cousin Dan and his wife for ten dollars a week, which covered my room and meals. That left me eighteen dollars a week to make the payment on my car which was thirty dollars a month, which left me forty two dollars a month for my personal needs. Gas was fourteen cents a gallon at the Red Bird station, and you could buy a home cooked plate lunch for seventy five cents a plate, which included your drink. These were the good old days that we will never see again. I worked for Pepsi Cola for three years and it prepared me with a certain toughness that has stayed with me my entire life.

Today we live in a world of many loafers who want something for nothing and many are too lazy to work for a living. They depend on the government to buy their food and pay their doctor bills. This is not what made America great and it will be the cause of our fall. It's by pain and hard work that our nation was formed and has become the Queen of the nations of the world. Today our streets are filled with gangs and dope traffic as well as sexual perverts that devour small children and rape our ladies. They grab ladies' purses in parking lots without any guilt even knocking them to the ground. Many streets in many cities are unsafe to walk on in broad daylight. Greed, lust, and pleasure mad people are what make up America, which we call the land of the free, and they will go to any length to satisfy their cravings.

Our hearts should weep as we view the dark clouds of sin and moral corruption that has engulfed our beloved, beautiful nation. In comparison to the memories of the good old days we are crowded with many unwelcome events here in the present. We search for a solution or a way of escape, but it only seems to worsen. Our prisons have become so crowded our civil courts are releasing many before they serve the time given for their crime, and millions are given probation without jail time for severe crimes. In the Bible David said, "The floods of ungodly men make me afraid." David, the man that could break the lion's jaw and slay the giant, was afraid. David knew what evil and ungodly men would do to any nation that flourished within it.

His words reach into this very hour that we live and we cry out with David. The evils that have engulfed our world make me afraid once again. What do we do? Where do we go? How do we handle it? The only answer is to turn to the God of the high heavens who is master of everything. To turn to the God who is in control, and never out of control. Only God is superior to the demons of evil that have possessed the minds of millions today.

Evil is of the devil and evil has no conscience or guilt of the horrible murders and attacks that we are seeing in humanity today worldwide. The great apostle Paul referred to the demons as, "Having their conscience seared by a hot iron." To me that means calloused beyond guilt as they bring hurt and pain to others. The craving for power and control has devoured moral conscience as the demon of greed controls many today. I hesitate to write the negative views of our nation, but it would make my story incomplete to not include the present day tone and condition of our nation that I and many others look upon with a troubled spirit.

As we make comparison to human responses from the good old days along with human responses today we find a contrast that brings clouds to our conscience and even guilt as we ask, "What have we done? Where shall we go from here?" Truly we have improved living conditions in our nation today by many inventions to a point of luxury and easy living. I would have to say these conditions beat the good old days all to pieces. However, there is another side to living that has nothing to do with material betterment or easy living and it is by far the most important.

Most important of all is the enforcement and protection of family and spiritual values. The decay and loss of these virtues has brought America to another definition in reputation. Human decency and reputation is constructed and upheld by the enforcement and dedication to family and spiritual values. Maybe we have opened the door and tossed these values out which would answer the question of why we have so many school shootings, gang fights, dope lords and sex maniacs who walk our streets and torture and murder our little children and our ladies. Something is wrong in America and in our world. I believe everyone would agree that something must be done to make our world a better and safer place to live. I hope people will take the responsibility to mind, as I have and realize that each one of us that works to restore family and spiritual values is the answer of restoration. Looking back to the good old days will not heal the sickness in our world today, but it might cause us to see the contrast of where we once were and where we are heading.

Today we live in a liberal and uncommitted generation as many of our young people live a wild and anything goes lifestyle. As soon as they get out from under the thumb of their parents by spending the night with friends, family values are left behind. Today our young people and some old as well, party all night and sleep all day with a dangerous and irresponsible attitude. Responsibility is a word that doesn't seem to be in their dictionary, in their quest of having a good time or as they plan their day. The fact is a day without fun is a dull day so fun should be included, but when it is all fun and no work, responsibility is left far behind.

We have often heard it said, "All work and no play is a dull day," maybe it should be rewritten as, "All play and no work creates a character that is an irresponsible jerk." Excuse me for my boldness. If the people of the good old days lived the same lifestyle, they would have milked cows at two in the afternoon and had breakfast at four.

Bus drivers who pick up children for school are familiar with the wave at the door from the mother signaling them to go on, for reasons such as the kids are late getting up, mom overslept from a hangover from the night before or watching the R-Rated late movie that she shouldn't be watching in the first place. Many parents in today's society support their children in irresponsible ways by living the same negative lifestyle before them.

Many in our nation today look for ways to lie around the house and live off our government by a free handout, when many of them are actually able to work and earn a living. Charity was an insult to most in the good old days because people took pride in providing for their own financial needs. These days of long ago have vanished by irresponsible and greedy people who depend on things like the lottery for their American dream.

Today we have child bosses in the home who whine and throw fits if things don't go their way while parents give in to their whims. The Bible says, "What manner of child is it that the father chastens not?" God doesn't mean to beat them, but I believe that to chasten means to instruct them with the true words of spiritual wisdom and enforce them by not taking no for an answer from the child.

In the days of old people worked at it to keep their family name a respected name and their reputation was important to them. Today respected reputations is not a part of the family plan as we see parents bail their children out of jail for drinking, using drugs, or breaking the law by other means. We can all see the change and where we are heading, but many shut their eyes and won't admit it. Today family values have vanished along with the good old days where families upheld house rules and Christian values. As I write these truths many will not like to be reminded of the terrible, negative conditions we find and have to face in America, but hiding from the sickness won't cure the disease. Of course all were not good stewards of family values and responsibilities in the good old days, but there was a much higher percentage of parents enforcing Godly and honorable family values and responsibilities then.

In the good old days who ever heard of even a suggestion not to pray in our public schools and class rooms? A suggestion like that would have stirred up a nest of hornets and the sting would have been felt far and wide. In the good old days who ever heard the likes of taking a tiny baby out of a mother's womb and killing it because of an unwanted pregnancy? Some pregnancies are accidental, or forced on our ladies, but it doesn't give anyone the right to kill a helpless tiny baby. It is still the mothers own blood and life giving elements that form the baby. This means it's her own flesh and blood which gives the baby life, and that makes it a blood relative.

To kill a fetus in the good old days would have been the most horrible crime you could commit and you would have been an outcast in your town. Today people walk our streets carrying signs on their back as they fight for the right to kill an innocent baby without guilt, and our government has signed a law giving permission to their evil desires of legalized abortion. Sex before marriage produces babies which are unwanted pregnancies. The proper thing for men and women to do is to face their responsibilities by getting married and raise their precious love child and their hearts will be glad as they watch their baby take its first steps and say its first words as it grows up. Murder should never be permitted in any form because the golden rule of God is, "Thou shall not kill".

Bullying of children by other children in our schools is causing mental and emotional damage to some and drives our children to suicide and mass murder. Our kids carry guns into classrooms and open fire for revenge on their classmates. Road rage across our nation because of congested traffic has caused fights and shootings just to get people out of their way. We live in a selfish age of pushing and shoving which has divorced human courtesy and respect of others. These few conditions we face today in this untoward generation blacken the image of family values and reputation that is far from the good old days of the past. The saying, "if you can't beat them, join them," I believe is what we are doing today. However, we need to pursue our convictions and stick to them. Convictions must have courage and by convictions and courage I believe each person can make our nation better by upholding family values that were taught to us in the good old days. It's better to make a friend than an enemy and our Bible tells us, "If a man desires a friend, let him show himself friendly."

As I go back in memory and view the conditions that I was part of I find a good reason to call them the good old days. In comparing the forties to this day of two thousand eleven there is a noticeable contrast in family values and the mental attitude of the people. I still believe good can overrule evil and giving is far more rewarding than taking. I still believe a smile toward a clouded countenance can brighten the day for a troubled spirit, and I believe that kindness returned to those who have wronged us is the stone of David that killed the mighty giant of evil. I still believe in family harmony and love in the mist of the rivers of evil men that trouble and press against our peace and liberty. I still believe in neighbors with helping hands and consideration, who share one another's burdens with compassion and love. When my cracker barrel is full and my neighbor has none to feed his family, I still find the spirit of sharing and words of encouragement. Sharing is caring, and caring is sharing.

Porch Swings and Neighbors

The good old days were filled with neighbors that cared for one another and shared in sorrow and hurt. In the good old days neighbors were friendly people we could borrow sugar, flour, or coffee from. I can remember many times Mother would send a cup of flour or sugar back to our neighbor that she had borrowed. Borrowing from one another was just being good neighbors, and good neighbors were common in those days. Most seemed eager to lend to a neighbor in need, and found joy in so doing. Times were hard and most understood the struggles of one another trying to make ends meet.

Almost everyone had a porch swing and since air conditioning was unheard of many would sit in their swings on a warm summer day to keep cool. As neighbors would walk by they would stop and chat for a while. They would inquire how everyone was, talk about the weather, about their hens that weren't laying as many eggs or maybe inquire about someone who had been sick. At times they would sit with you on the porch and talk small talk for hours. If there was not time to stop and chat they would always give a friendly wave and call you by name as they passed by. Today porch swings are missing with air conditioned homes and hundreds of television channels to select from, not to mention two or three computers in most homes. Today the friendly waves of passing neighbors are missing and where there are porch swings, most of them are empty.

As far as neighbors go now, many don't even know who lives on their block. Also, with the abundance of sugar, flour, coffee and credit cards to buy with, who needs neighbors anyway? The fact is a modern world has taken away a neighboring lifestyle that will never return. The empty porch swings only remind us that the good old days of friendly neighbors are gone and now six foot privacy fences form walls of separation to keep neighbors from stealing yard ornaments out of our yards.

Evil men have caused us to be withdrawn from friendliness because a next door neighbor could be our worst enemy. Lust, drugs, and drink have changed our neighborhoods to a very unsafe environment. Today because of evil men we view our neighbors as those who stand in harm's way, and so friendliness has turned into resentment. We must remember and never forget that Jesus said to love your neighbor as yourself. This means we should care for their souls and offer to them the same peace and love that we find in Jesus. Good neighbors should maintain a forgiving spirit and always have the compassion and desire to be a good neighbor by loving and caring for them that are lost.

Before my wife, Fran, and I were saved and started going to church regularly we would meet at our neighbors every weekend and play music, drink, sing, and party. Then we would sleep in on Sunday morning with a hangover and seldom ever go to church. That all changed after Jesus came into our lives, we had a new desire and all the old habits were gone, no more drinking and no more all night parties. When my neighbor found out we were saved and going to church regularly, he told me he lost a good neighbor. I replied no, and told him he had gained a good neighbor. Before I was limited because of sin but now I can be a better neighbor. Little did I know at that time that one day soon I would answer the call to preach the Gospel and a few years later baptize that very neighbor and his wife that we once spent our nights with drinking and living in sin.

Just this past year the family of my past neighbor called me to preach each of their funerals, and there was a certain joy as I realized my wife and I had a part in leading our neighbors to Jesus. How sad it would have been if we would have resented them like the Pharisees in the Bible, and very possibly they could have went into eternity without finding their way to salvation. Following Jesus has been an adventure of joy and I wouldn't give one minute of it for all the world's pleasures combined.

In the early days we had another neighbor whose dog killed their neighbor's chickens. The neighbor, who lost the chickens, asked a fellow neighbor what the Bible says about how you are to treat your neighbors. The neighbor replied, "It says, do unto him as he does unto you," and so he went and shot the man's dog. Jesus gives us the true virtues of love where our neighbors are concerned when He said, "Love your neighbor as yourself." I wonder how many bad relationships would have been avoided if they would have followed this principal? Of course our Lord revealed His own heart of true compassion for all men when He said that, and He proved it when He said, "Father forgive them, for they know not what they do." He, the great example, is the pattern for me. Jesus loves all men in spite of their rejection of His life. How much better our neighborhoods would be if men would follow and accept the words of our Lord and savior Jesus Christ, "Love thy neighbor as thyself."

My prayer today is, Lord, bring back that spirit in us to rebuild family values that are best defined by one word; LOVE. Help us to love our neighbor as ourselves and to turn away from the direction we are heading until one day men will look back at this generation and say, "Remember the good old days of two thousand eleven."

I look at the path of the apostles and see the blood washed and spirit filled, who gave of themselves for the good of others. The sands of the eastern world are stained with their blood as they gave the ultimate gift for the kingdom of God. In their steadfastness for good we see in contrast, those who fight against God and His anointed and follow the path of evil. Although Christians are vastly outnumbered they are walking the path that leads to victory, and in the final battle they will be the victors as Jesus drives back the forces of evil. One day soon Jesus will stand on the bow of the world and He will say once again, "Peace, be still," and there will be a great calm that will never be turbulent again forever throughout eternity.

As Christians we gain courage as we walk hand in hand with Jesus who is the master of the storm, and we know that He placed the bow in the clouds for a divine reminder that He is with those who follow Him, He goes before His sheep clearing the way where obstacles often block the way. When the way is dark He sends a beacon of light to keep our feet in the path that leads to our eternal home. Truly, He will never leave us nor forsake us.

Every time we stand in the dark shadows of life we find Jesus standing nearby, for He doesn't leave his children unattended. We must never forget, Jesus is on our side, and He wants us to make it to heaven. He is not trying to make the way harder, but He makes the way possible. We could reach no destination without His directions, and Jesus has given us clear detail and a well marked map in His holy word that leads all the way to glory.

In the next section I will move from a small boy and teenager to adulthood. In the pages ahead I will relate the ministry that God has called me to with the many experiences I witnessed in the ministry. The following chapters in this book is a true account of events that have brought blessing to my soul as I go back in time and revisit in memory the path of my life. I pray that others will find faith in the same measure that I have as I revisit true events of my past. Life itself is our greatest teacher of learning, and past memories can be our best friend. I remember it like yesterday as I continue the path that started at a time in history that we call the good old days.

CHAPTER TWO

A Change in Life

In this chapter the memories will be laced with spiritual blessings that I wish to share with you that relate to my thirty five years of pasturing and preaching the gospel. It all started in a little village called Augusta, which is located in Southern Indiana. This is where my wife and I bought our first home where we raised our three children. Life was good, I had a good job at Whirlpool Corporation and our property had plenty of garden space where I raised a large garden, and Fran would can lots of our vegetables for the long winter. We had all we needed but somehow we could never get our head above water. Bills would pile up, we would overdraw at the bank, and we were always in a struggle to make ends meet. I was selfish and lived my life as if life was only for me.

My weekends were planned to what I wanted to do and I gave very little consideration to my wife and children. Every Sunday I would go to the gym and play basket ball until I was wore out. Then there was fishing, hunting, and horseback riding. I played softball in the summer along with basketball. It was plain to see that I was selfishly leaving the family out of my life as I would plan every weekend to fit my plans. I seldom ever went to church because I thought I had better things to do, but one day all of that was to change. I had Christian parents and they prayed for God to move into my life and wake me up from where I was heading. Mom often pleaded for me to take my family to church, and one day when she asked me to go to church I told her something I wish I hadn't. I told her to go to church because she was old and already had all her fun, and that I was still young and wanted to have fun like she did. If I could speak to mother again I would thank her for hanging in there for me, even when I hurt her with my words.

For about five years, I betted on horses through a bookie at the plant where I worked. I became a compulsive gambler. Sometimes I would win but most of the time I would lose. One day mom told me she was praying that my horses would lose, and I told her she should pray that they would win because I needed the money for my family. I'll never forget those next few days at the race track. I had horses to win by ten lengths, but were disqualified and placed last. There were times the horse would break out the gate and the jockey fell off, and times the horse that I bet on ran into the fence and broke its leg. There were also times they would have a pile up and my horse always seemed to be in the pile. As I think back I believe it was God at work answering mother's prayers. I remember losing my entire vacation money one summer while Fran and the children were waiting at home to leave for it. I managed to go, but I had to borrow the money from my neighbor.

When God has a plan for your life he will do whatever it takes to activate your life to do His will. Jesus came by our home in a blessed way, as our ten year old son lay in the hospital at the point of death; it stopped me in my tracks. Guilt overwhelmed me like I had never faced it before. I was a sinner and I needed to pray for my son, but the guilt was so heavy I figured God wouldn't hear me for the way that I had treated Him my whole life. Then I realized my need and I prayed the prayer of repentance and Jesus forgave me of my sins. Now a light had turned on in my soul from heaven and I knew God was real in it. God spared my son even after the doctor had told us he might not live to morning. Our son, Rick, now has three children in a Christian college and he is principal of an elementary school. Not only is he principal but he is a Christian as well.

I am sure Mother had good reason to pray for her children, and prayers answered are real to Fran and me today. No earthly ambition in this whole world could turn my love for God. I have found a peace that the world never gave. Fran and I joined our church and was elected as officers on the church board and served in that capacity for five years. Then on February sixth 1976, God called me to preach the gospel. This would take me on a journey that I would have never dreamed I would take. I enrolled in the course of study for ministers and my pastor issued my first ministers licenses, and almost immediately I begin supply preaching at area churches.

As soon as we became Christians, God used our witness as a way to affect people in our neighborhood. One Sunday morning we were getting ready to go to church and I noticed our neighbor lady sitting in our front yard in one of our lawn chairs. She was known as the town grouch, she would even shoot her neighbors' dogs if they got in her yard. Most of the people didn't like her and she lived alone. She was nearly eighty years old. I walked over to where she was sitting and said, "Good morning, can I help you?" She asked me if we went to a little church in Winslow, and I told her we did. She told me she thought she would ride to church with my family if I didn't mind. I told her we would be happy to take her to church with us. And so she came for a few Sundays. A few weeks later we got word that she had cancer and was in the hospital and they didn't expect her to live. Fran and I went to her bedside and asked her if she would like to be a Christian. She said she would so we prayed with her and she made her peace with God. In just a few days, she went to be with the Lord.

One of our next door neighbors was my old drinking buddy. We fished together, hunted together, and played music many nights all night long along with the drinking until I became a Christian. Many years passed but we stayed in contact with them across the years. One day we were sitting at home and the phone rang, it was our neighbors. They wanted me to baptize them because they had gotten saved. I believe that is the best way to love your neighbor as yourself, that is, to tell them about Jesus and about salvation.

During those early days as a Christian, God used my family to win others for Christ. Our daughter, Debbie, began dating another neighbor and the rule was that he would have to go to church with us. I remember kneeling at the altar with him as he gave his heart to the Lord. Within a few months he was helping cut timber when tree fell on him and took him to be with Jesus. I believe when one turns to God others will follow, and I shudder in my soul to think what if I had not minded God. Where would my family and I be today? Where would our neighbors be that found the Lord through our witness in those early days as a Christian?

People may not think life as a Christian means much in this corrupted world, but I believe that God uses every Christian on the face of the earth to be His witnesses and to be an earthly light to those that are lost. All who walk through life without Jesus in their heart or in their home or who don't attend church will see many unhappy endings. Sin has no happy endings and those who walk in sin will suffer all the heartbreak that surely goes with it.

The Bible says, "How shall we escape if we neglect so great a salvation." There is only one path where the sun is always shining whether it is dark and rainy or bright and sunny, because the sun never fails to shine in the heart where Jesus reigns. Paul said, "Christ in you the hope of glory. Greater is He that is in me than he that is in the world. If Christ be for us, who can be against us," and also, "Who shall separate us from the love of God." If that isn't enough, Jesus himself said, "I am the good shepherd and the good shepherd stands by his sheep." That puts us in a class where His Angels are encamped round about us.

The song lyrics say, "If Jesus goes with me I'll go anywhere." I believe I know where that song writer was coming from. When David rushed forth to meet the giant his frail body didn't stop him as he cried out to all, "I come in the name of the Lord!" When envisioning the falling giants that stand before us we are living by faith in the one that has all power and authority. The one that will remove the obstacles out of our path and shine a light before us to keep our feet on the road that leads to glory. Jesus never fails and the only safe place on earth is in His loving hands. Give it all to Him and one day He will give it all to you. If you believe that with me say "AMEN" good and loud.

The passion for the lost that was within my heart became stronger with each passing day and I knew it was time to find a church where God could use me and also to prepare myself to be at my best for Jesus. So, I enrolled in a Bible school that was located in the mountains of Eastern Kentucky and at the same time agreed to pastor one of their small mountain churches. This would be mine and my wife's first church that we would pastor and it turned out to be our learning station as we witnessed the hand of God leading us and teaching us the way of the cross. We were taught what it means to live by faith and our many experiences that God brought us through gave us a true definition of it. A journey without faith is a useless one and a complete failure because where there is no faith the vision is blurred and we can't see beyond the heavy clouds before us. But where faith rules, it has x ray vision enabling us to see through the walls of dark and heavy clouds that so often stand before us. Real faith can see the invisible and knows that although we can't see Him we know that Jesus is just beyond the dark walls of opposition and that He will stand by us whatever the battle may be. So we walk into the dark clouds with the banner of faith in our hand lifted high in the name of the Lord.

Before this next chapter I wish to share with you a message on faith. It was faith that brought hope into our world and helped us to look up in our despair. Each of us must hold fast to faith in the living God as we travel this uncertain path. The good old days would have been a sad vision to look back on if the folks that lived them were without faith. Their faith was their strongest weapon and their source of courage that pushed them on through many trials and disappointments. Please share with me as we look back to the days of Elijah the Prophet and find a great act of faith from the old Prophet as he prayed for rain at a time of terrible drought and famine. Elijah's act of faith was rewarded by God and the rains came down upon the dry ground in abundance. His message on faith is crucial to the remaining chapters of this book. With it, it will be like wearing glasses to improve our dim vision to see more clearly that FAITH IS THE VICTORY.

(1-Kings 18:41-45) And Elijah said unto Ahab, "get thee up, eat and drink; for there is a sound of abundance of rain." So Ahab went up to eat and to drink. And Elijah went up to the top of Carmel, and he cast himself down upon the earth, and put his face between his knees, and said to his servant, "go up now, look toward the sea." And he went up and looked, and said, "There is nothing." Then Elijah said, "Go again seven times." And it came to pass at the seventh time that he said, "Behold there arises a little cloud out of the sea like a man's hand," and Elijah said, "get thee down that the rain stop thee not." And it came to pass in the meanwhile that the heaven was black with clouds and wind, and there was a great rain. Elijah's servant must have thought he was wasting his time about the third or fourth trip and I can imagine he said to Elijah things like it's no use, there isn't a cloud in the sky, but reluctantly the servant went back the seventh trip. Elijah stayed on his knees and when a small cloud appeared it didn't help the servant much, but Elijah knew the rain was coming. When Elijah prayed in faith the heavens were moved as God intervened and there was a great rain in the land.

Real faith can see the sunlight in the middle of a dark storm because we know that the almighty God sends the rain as well as the sunlight, and He holds it all in His hand of power. Sometimes we may feel that we are all alone when the way gets rough and rugged, but I have learned when we walk through a dark and deep valley if we listen closely we will hear footsteps beside us because Jesus said, "I will never leave thee nor forsake thee." That's a promise that will never be broken and if you are failing to hear the footsteps beside you down in your deep valley, your faith has been tampered with by the devil.

When faith is real you will hear not only footsteps beside you, but you will hear the still, small voice of encouragement in your darkest moments. Jesus often commended those in the Bible who showed strong faith. He said, "Thy faith has made you whole," and many were healed. Another time Jesus said, "I have not seen such faith in all the land," and He met the people's needs. But, Jesus also rebuked those who were weak in faith. When the disciples were in a boat with Jesus and a terrible wind begin to threaten they cried out to Jesus, "Master care thou not that we perish," and Jesus said, "Oh ye of little faith… Peace be still," and there was a great calm. Faith is always rewarded, but we grieve the spirit when faith is weak.

There are two sets of eyes where faith is concerned; one will see dimly through the fog, and the other will see no fog. For example: There were two men in prison and as they looked out through the bars of the jail, one said look at the mud while the other said look at the stars how brightly they shine. To me this symbolizes weak and strong faith because conditions were bad for both men but one revealed a positive mind of faith because he could see beauty beyond the mud and the valley they were in. When our faith is real our vision will see the beauty and positive things of God's grace.

Rainbows are hidden by weak faith, but when faith is real the colors of the rainbow are brilliant. The fact is we must see beyond the rainbows in life much more than just a rainbow. We must hear the promises of God as He whispers with that still small voice, "Fear not for low I am with thee even unto the end of the world." When we see with eyes of faith, how much clearer the rainy days become. A negative vision that can only see all the problem's that surround them will bring pain to the soul. But, a positive vision of faith can always see the light at the end of the tunnel. Where faith rules there is no amount of dark clouds that can hide the beauty of the sunlight.

The song says, "The clouds cannot hide His blessed face." Faith was not born by some empty fantasy or imaginary fictional character, but faith is born in our hearts vision of an unseen guest that lives in our hearts who is supreme in power and authority. Even the wind and the waves obey His will. His love is fresh everyday when we need someone to love us and embrace us. When we fall on our knees and pray for pressing issues, may we see Elijah's small cloud by looking up away from the weight of our burdens that overload our human effort and crowd around our life. May we see the strong shoulder of the Lord assisting us as He bares the weight with His own shoulder of love. When we do, the heavy loads of life become lighter as faith takes hold. It is by faith in God we walk through the rugged path of life with spring in our steps, and the evils that so often surround us fall to the side as Jesus clears the way before us. Jesus is the Captain of our salvation, and He is qualified to lead us through earthly obstacles that stand in our path.

Not only does Jesus clear our path but He shines a beacon of light before of us to show us the way and keep us in route to that blessed city where He waits to welcome His children home. The word of God is the eternal light that marks the way well that we not get off the route. If any man fails to make it to Heaven it will be because he did not follow the well marked path that God made visible by the prophets and preachers of many generations. Paul has well said, "Thou art inexcusable." Ezekiel said, "Why will ye die, turn ye, turn ye, and live."

Today the gospel light continues to shine in a dark and violent world where immoral permissiveness has engulfed it. Millions are lost in the storms of sin that rages like a roaring river, but yet God still keeps the lighthouse burning, and its lights still sweeps across the stormy seas where many are drifting and lost in the winds of Satan. Our faith should hear the words of Jesus when He stood on the bow of the boat in a raging storm and said," Peace be still," and there was a great calm. Soon Jesus will once again stand on the bow of this old world and say those words and once again forever there will be a great calm. Satan and all evil men will fall aside into the great lake of fire where they will be held in chains of darkness forever. They preferred darkness in this life so God will give them the desires of their hearts in eternity.

Today a glorious light is shining in the path of every person on earth giving direction to a place called Heaven. God is still calling to the lost sheep on a thousand hills to come home. His voice is pleading and filled with love because He knows that He will soon have to turn all the lighthouses out and those who are drifting on the seas of sin will be lost forever. God has sent His ministers into the dense jungles of darkness all over the world and many of them have been killed by evil men with their Bible yet in their hand. But still, God leaves the lights burning and calls out to the lost to come home.

I have spoke from the depths of my soul concerning faith in God and how faith can bring peace in our life and in our homes. It is by faith that we are saved and it is by faith that we can endure life's most trying moments. Faith will open the closed doors before us and give us spring in our step as we journey on toward that glorious and blessed city of God where the light will shine forever and not a dark day will ever come. In Him is no darkness at all and our faith in Him will turn on the lights for our journey that lies ahead of us giving us clear vision up the path to Glory. Praise His Holy name forever!

Our faith in God will kill the giants, cool the flaming furnaces, close the mouth of lions, break the keepers on prison doors, and part the waters giving passage to God's children into Canaan land that lies in the city of God forever. Faith's eye sees through the dense fog of life a bright and glorious future that lies in the New Jerusalem where the redeemed will reside with Jesus forevermore.

Included in the good old days was spiritual education which was very important to most of the people. In our home many evenings Mother would read us the Bible and always pray after she would read. I was in church at the age of four every Sunday and I sometimes am surprised at things I remember that was taught to me at such a young age. The most important part of life in this old world today is Christian training. With the present age of turmoil and murderous dictators, Christians are being killed and this very moment and evil beliefs are being forced on them. It is not a choice but an order in many areas of the world. The need has never been greater for our children to be taught the true Gospel of Jesus Christ than it is today.

Classrooms in our schools are forbidden to teach Christianity to children in any form because of the church and state rules. This leaves it totally up to parents to teach their children about Jesus and about salvation. I am so glad that a change came into our home at a very young age for us children and we were all taught in church, as well as, at home the story of Jesus and many other Bible stories. When Mother and Dad gave their hearts to God in 1941, they were very sincere. Up until the day they went to be with Jesus, they were still holding on in true faith. How different my life would have been had it not been for the faithfulness of Mother and Dad. It has not only led me into the ministry but it has helped me to raise my children under the influence of Christian people within the body of the Church.

PART TWO

OUR
MOUNTAIN JOURNEY

CHAPTER THREE
Our Mountain Journey

REV. ROBERT KING
Campton, KY

MRS. FRANCIES KING
Campton, KY

It was a Sunday morning 1972 and as usual we slept late not even thinking about going to church. Our three children as well were snuggled up in bed, Kim, our oldest child was 14, Deb was 12, and our only son, Rick, who was 10. Life was good. I had a good job, a home and two automobiles which made it convenient for me to plan my weekends. I loved to hunt, fish, ride my horse, and play basketball. Sunday was my day for personal pleasures and fun, I simply had no time for God. However, on this particular Sunday, God was going to step in and change my selfish lifestyle forever.

I had gone to the gym at Stendal, Indiana to play basketball with my friends which I wouldn't miss for any reason. We had just gotten started when my neighbor came to the gym with a message. He told me they had rushed my son Rick to the Hospital and they were preparing to do emergency surgery. I rushed to the hospital and found out that Rick had a ruptured appendix. They were preparing him for surgery when I arrived at the hospital. They did the surgery and the doctor took us to a room to explain what they had done. He told us it was very bad, and that he might not live till morning.

Rick was in intensive care and fighting for his life. Having been raised in the church, I knew we needed God to intervene. I was standing by his bed side in intensive care and his face was as white as a bed sheet. My heart dropped, I felt helpless for the first time in my life. I needed to pray, but the guilt was so heavy from the way I had been treating God I just knew He wouldn't listen to me. I went back into the waiting room, walked over to the window which was on the second floor of the hospital and looked out across the tops of the houses. The first thing I saw was a church steeple sticking up with a white cross on top. My eyes were drawn to it like a magnet as I stared my eyes became frozen to the cross. God spoke to my heart and I knew what I must do. I asked God to forgive me of my sins which were many and standing there with my eyes fixed on the cross, its purpose became reality and Jesus met my need.

On May the seventh, 1972, I met the Master and I knew my sins were under the blood. I went back into the intensive care unit by Rick's bedside. He looked up at me and said, "Daddy I'm scared." I assured him that he was going to be alright, that God was helping. Then I thought about how he was 10 years old and maybe he should ask God to forgive him of his sins as well. In my heart I thought if he was to die, and perhaps he was old enough to give account, maybe he should pray. I looked down at his little white face and I said, "Rickey sometimes we do some bad things and maybe you should ask God to forgive you." He looked up at me and said, "Daddy, I already did."

I remember that moment as it were just yesterday that wonderful warmth flowed through me and a peace I'll never forget. I made a vow to God that day that if He would spare my son I would make sure my family was in Church. After over thirty days in the hospital the fever broke and Rick was released from the hospital and we went home. As I had promised, we attended Church for a while, but when Rick became completely healed we quit going. In just a few weeks he became very sick again will all the same symptoms. We rushed him to the doctor and they had to do exploratory surgery immediately. My guilt was large. I knew I had broken my vow to God so I begin to pray and ask Him to forgive me and spare my son. I prayed and told God that from now on as long as I live I'll not only take my family to Church, but I would serve Him and follow His will. Fran came into the waiting room about that time and I said to her that unless we both give our hearts to the Lord I don't believe Rick will get better. She said, "I already did."

God gave us back our son that day. He is a merciful God and He cares for each of us with an equality and unconditional love. Later Fran told me how she had prayed and told the Lord that even if He didn't spare our son she would still serve Him. That's the stone that killed the giant. God's will, should always have first priority as we pray.

Shortly after Rick's second trip to the hospital, Fran and I became very active in the Church Of The Nazarene in Winslow, Indiana. We served as teachers, young people's president, Sunday School Superintendant, and were on the Church board for about five years. During those years God called me to preach the Gospel, and so my Pastor issued me a local license to preach at our church occasionally. Then I enrolled in the course of study for ministers and begin my studies immediately. This led us to continue our studies in a Bible School in Eastern Kentucky. The years have passed fast, and the entire thirty five years I preached God has always kept an open door for Fran and I to serve in His blessed Kingdom. There are too many miles behind me to give up now or to turn back. God's call on my life to preach His Gospel came on Feb. 6, 1976, and immediately I begin this blessed journey.

God has enriched my life these past thirty five years and guided me through many blessed experiences. I feel led by God to put many of these events in writing so that others might find the joy and blessings that God has given Fran and me across the years. The sacrifices and struggles have been many, but they have always ended in blessings. I think of the words of the song *No One Ever Cared for Me like Jesus,* no one ever was so kind as he.

We began our spiritual journey by enrolling in the course of study for Ministers in the Church of the Nazarene. I completed several courses, but I felt I needed something more. Some friends that we made while Rick was in the hospital told us of a very special school in Eastern Kentucky. They told us there was no place on earth with such spiritual and dedicated people, and that we just had to go for a visit and see for ourselves. We made some inquires concerning the Bible College and we liked what we found out.

At that time our daughter Kim felt Gods call on her life, and she was accepted into the Bible School, Kentucky Mountain Bible Institute. It wasn't long before I felt very strongly that God was leading me to attend the Bible College. So I wrote a letter to Dr. Paulo who was president of the association. His answer came back and he said he had met with the executive committee and that the vote was unanimous for us to come and be a part of their group. This included a small church to pastor with a nice parsonage for our family to live in and it was only fifteen miles from the campus. Dr. Paulo informed us that by pastoring the church it would pay for both our tuitions. We were amazed as we watched God's hand prepare the way before us.

Without any incomes it would have been impossible to attend without the open door that the good people gave to us. We had owned a small farm house with four acres that we loved very much. I had said I would never sell it because it was the home where we raised our children into their teenage years, but the only way we could possibly attend the Bible College was to sell our home that we loved so much and clear our debts. So we ran an ad in the paper and in a few days a family came and wanted to buy it. We priced it for $20,000 and they agreed, but could only borrow $15,000. We told them that we couldn't possibly take any less than $20,000, but the very next day I got the idea that if we could keep one acre we could let them have it for $15,000. I hurried home from work and told Fran what I had come up with and asked her what she thought. Her answer made me stop and think. She asked if remembered those people in the Bible who held back part of the money and failed to mind God. I said I remembered, and she then told me believed we needed to let them have it all for $15,000 because we were not going to need it any more working, for the Lord. And so they bought our place.

The next thing to do was quit my job at Whirlpool Corp. of fourteen years which was a very good job with three weeks paid vacation and good medical coverage for my family. So I went to the office and told the personnel manager I was quitting and I needed to freeze my accredited seniority for retirement years. I'll never forget her answer. She asked why I don't take a leave of absence instead of quitting in case I don't make it in the ministry. She told me of how hard it is to get people into Church, and that a leave of absence would let me come back and reclaim my job. I said, "No ma'am you don't understand. I have no choice and there is no going back. I have to make it work." So while filling out my pink slip, she looked up and asked what to write down for reason for leaving. I answered, "For other employment," and I later wrote on the slip, "Employed by Jesus Christ."

We got our money for our house, paid off all our debts and were left with $2,100.00. With that we left for the mountains of Eastern Kentucky. We were on our way at last, and everyone was excited. I'll never forget that cold December day as we left Southern Indiana. Before loading up, Fran had to go to town and on the way home she spun the car around on the icy road. Luckily, God was there and straightened the car out without having to call the towing service. Then we rented a large Ryder truck and loaded everything we had on it. Friends of ours, Jerry and Sharon Austin, agreed to drive it for us so they drove all the way to our parsonage in Campton Kentucky.

As we prepared to leave, Jerry backed the truck into a ditch and its bank was so steep it looked as if the truck would turn over at any minute. We called the Quick Bro. towing service, and with God's help we were able to get the truck back on the road. Finally we were on our way to serve the Lord in the ministry. It was sleeting and freezing rain the whole trip and we watched as several cars slid off the road and ended up ditches. We prayed through the entire trip and I believe God's mighty arms held us on course.

Our children had never seen the mountains and they were anxiously straining their eyes to see the first ones. Finally the mountains appeared and we all enjoyed the scenery. There it was finally, the sign we had been looking, the one that read 'Campton'. We then followed the directions that had been given to us which led us three miles out of Campton into the mountains. Then we finally saw it, sitting in the midst of a mountain valley, a beautiful little church with a tin roof and bell tower. Just like you'd see it on a Christmas card all covered with falling snow. Our first pastorate, we were finally there. Joy filled our hearts as we realized we had reached the place where God had opened the door for Fran and I to pursue God's calling. Jerry and Sharon helped us unload the truck and they spent the night. They were instrumental in helping us to get started in our first pastorate. We thank God for their kindness and willingness to lend a hand. As they left the next day we bid them good bye and prayed that God would give them a safe trip home.

We finished unpacking the next morning. It was just a couple of days until Sunday and we could hardly wait. The next day there was a spiritual moment I'll always remember. Fran and I and our three children went into the church and we sat down in the second pew from the front. There, we all sang together, "I'll go where you want me to go dear Lord, over mountain or plain or sea, I'll say what you want me to say dear Lord, I'll be what you want me to be. But if by a still, small voice He calls, to paths that I do not know, I'll answer, Dear Lord, with my hand in Thine, I'll go where you want me to go." A sweet spirit settled down around us as we sang out of our hearts. We had prayer and went back to our parsonage which was now our new home.

Then Came the Snow

It was December 1977, one of the worst winters we had seen in years. It snowed, and snowed, and snowed some more. I would clean off the walk to the Church, and the next morning it would be covered again. This went on for several weeks and we begin to think we were never going to get to have our first service. Finally the day arrived we were going to finally have church. Several showed up for that first service and it was wonderful as we all begin to sing. There is something magic in a mountain holler when you ring the church bell, and the people sing. The sound carried all across the mountain valley. I would always pull the rope a few extra times because to me that was calling to the needy to come and dine.

That first Sunday I preached on 'Being Identified with Christ,' and I felt I had totally bumped my head. There was no way, they surely wouldn't want me to be their pastor. As we dismissed the service a man came to the front where I was standing and shook my hand and said, "Thank you, we want you to be our pastor." My spirit was lifted and I was ready to face the next service.

Our First Offering

Fran and I counted our first offering; it was three dollars and eighty seven cents. Fran looked at me and I looked at her. I reminded her that the church and parsonage were heated by oil, and we had an electric bill. I asked her how in the world were we going to make it. Of course the enemy wasted no time in reminding me that I gave up a good job, moved out to a poverty area, and I didn't even know how to preach very well. I had thought put in my head like, 'you better load up and get back to Indiana before you and your children starve to death,' and, 'these people could care less about you. They are just a bunch of strangers, why should they care anyway.' We knew that our money wouldn't last very long and we would be in trouble, but somehow in our hearts we knew that the God that had placed us here would work it out and supply our needs.

We were getting very low on money when Fran and I went to the store in Campton. We stood in front of the meat box and I commented on the nice hams and how I sure would like to have one. Fran answered that we couldn't afford one. I replied, "We would have to buy it on payments if we got one." We just laughed and finished getting a few things then returned home. As soon as we got home I went to the mailbox and I couldn't believe my eyes. In a neatly wrapped package was the prettiest pink sliced ham I had ever laid eyes on. This gesture was the beginning of faith in a stronger measure in our service to God that carried us across these many years.

The Church grew and people were getting saved and sanctified as well. The offerings grew each week and we were managing to keep the bills paid and give us a small salary. A nice lady who owned a restaurant in Campton called and wanted to buy all the fuel for our church van. She bought it for the entire time of our ministry in the mountains of Eastern Kentucky. We found this to be true, "God will never send you where He will not furnish you the grace to go on." When God said, "The Just shall live by faith," he meant just exactly what he said. When your faith kicks in, in the big valleys, they disappear and you cross them in joy. I've often said when the mountains which appear in front of you look bigger than God's ability to move them, you have lost faith. Never forget; God has the ability to go where we can't go, and reach where we can't reach. I am often reminded of my limitations, but God has no limits or boundaries.

As Christians we each must believe that our God is able to remove every obstacle that Satan places in our path. We must see God bigger than every obstacle we face in life's journey, and when we do, we go forward. When we pray the prayer of faith we advance, but by our silence we retreat. Prayer is our weapon that every Christian has that will make the devil tremble and will draw grace from Heaven to go on.

The Work Begins

It was only a tiny little Church hid away in the mountains called Bear Pen Community Church, but God found it and visited it often. We had only been there a few weeks when I began to have severe headaches from a deteriorated disk in my lower back. My right leg all the way from my back on down, had pain that was unbearable. We tried everything, but there was no relief, it only seemed to get worse. Finally I went over to the church, fell across the altar and I prayed for God's touch. I prayed, "Dear Lord, if I'm going to be a pastor I'm going to need a clear head and a strong back."

God already knew what I needed, but I think sometimes He wants us to exercise our faith in Him before he touches our need. Well, I prayed but nothing happened. I slowly walked back into the parsonage and asked Fran to run hot water in the bathtub. I thought maybe a hot soak would help. I no sooner stepped my feet into the water when something happened that was like electricity running up and down my leg. God healed the pain instantly. I've never had another back attack or a severe headache these past thirty five years that we have served in the ministry.

I have pastured five churches, organized and played softball on our team, and held down many jobs across the years to support my family. I was able to do all this because God put healing power into my body. I even ran an ad in the paper to mow lawns and I ended up with thirteen lawns to mow every summer I spent in Campton, Ky. I used a push mower and some lawns were so steep I wore baseball spikes to keep from slipping. I must have walked a million miles for my Jesus. God gave me a job and an old mower that just kept right on going. I don't ever remember having to have it repaired. Isn't that just like Sanctification? All who have it run a whole lot smoother.

I think of the words in the book of Isaiah (40:31). *But, they that wait upon the Lord shall renew their strength, they shall mount up with the wings of Eagles, they shall run and not be weary, and they shall walk and not faint.* Praise God from whom all blessings flow. It wouldn't be right to go on without mentioning that as I write these blessings I am seventy three years old and I'm on no medication and rarely am I sick. My Doctor says my visits are social rather than a physical need. I thought if he only knew the whole story, all the years that God has stood by us, and all the hard places He has brought us through. I have a record that I like to share with people that I'm very proud of; I went seventeen years without missing a Sunday morning service. God has answered that simple prayer I prayed back in that little Mountain Church many times over.

One Sunday I was just too sick to go to church and I really hated to break my record. But, I learned that even the strongest men sometimes fall in battle, and maybe it's to remind us that our strength is in the Lord and we should never take God for granted. I believe God wants to have a daily relationship with all His children and that God has a way to keep us aware of His unseen presence. Sometimes we have to get down before we can truly look up and be still and know that He alone is God. When the test comes in a definite way and we are at our big valley may we respond like Job who never lost sight of God. When things couldn't have been worse, Job said, "I know my Redeemer lives, and though skin worms devour me yet will I trust in Him." Real faith never loses sight of God no matter how dark the day.

Springtime in the Mountains

When winter ended, spring unfolded its beauty across the mountain valleys with Easter lilies in bloom, and the song birds singing their sweet notes. All of nature spread its beauty before our eyes. The beauty of spring in the Mountains almost takes your breath away.

The long winter had finally ended and the roads were now passable to explore. It was now time to find folks to tell them about Jesus and invite them to church. So we began the work with more energy and expectancy. I began searching the mountains for people to come to our church and also to get acquainted with them. I soon found that the needs were great and that many needed Jesus in their life. The challenge stood before me and we began the work.

Mud Road and Log Houses

Mary Dunn who taught the smaller children Sunday School asked me to call on two sisters who lived past her house, down a dirt road in a mountain valley. I walked the dirt road, through the woods about three or four blocks, and I found a log house where the two elderly sisters lived alone. Their names were Flossie and Pearl. Pearl was disabled and in a wheel chair and her sister Flossie cared for her night and day. They were both near eighty years of age. The women assured me that they were Christians and they were very glad for me to visit with them in their home.

About two weeks later we started a Revival and I took them a Revival bill. I told Flossie that I realized she couldn't come, but that they could pray for the services. Pearl spoke up immediately and told Flossie she could go if she wanted to, and that she'd be alright till Flossie got home. So I drove the church van to their house the opening night to pick up Flossie who was as excited as a little child and ready to go. There was a picture window facing their driveway that we pushed Pearl's wheelchair in front of so she could watch for us to get home. When we got home she was still watching out the window. It was a lonely picture indeed.

At the service a smile never left Flossie's face and as the children sing she clasped her hands together. Her face was glowing. She was in church for the first time in years and her spiritual hunger for fellowship revealed her heart's need. God made a way for one of His children to be in church when there had been no way. After church when we arrived at her home, she got out of the van, thanked me and headed toward her front steps. I waited to insure that she got in the house safely. I was amazed at what I saw. She was too weak to climb the steps so she got down on her knees and literally crawled up them onto the porch. Our trip had totally worn her out.

I went out to check on Pearl and Flossie the next day and suggested that Flossie rest a night or two before she went back to church. She immediately disagreed. She said, "I wouldn't miss it for the world. I want to go every night," and so she did. From then on when I took her home I used their back door and walked her in her house through it, where there was only one step to get into the house. Ever since that day Flossie crawled up her front porch steps, I've wondered why people stay home from Church for such small reasons.

I believe the love of God in our soul is revealed by our desire to support His Kingdom. We find that the Disciples were steadfast, unmovable always abounding in the work of the Lord. Nothing could turn them from their duty to God. We have their record in God's Holy Word. Our joy should be at its best when we have done something for God.

One day when I was visiting Flossie's home, she asked me if I would call on her sister-in-law who lived on the same road just before Flossie's house. I wasted no time and stopped by on my way home. She was very nice and invited me into her home. I invited her to our church and she said she wasn't very well and she wouldn't promise me anything. A few days later I stopped in to visit her again and she was on her porch crying. She had just gotten a report back from the doctor that she had cancer. That was all I needed to hear to talk to her about her soul. I can still see her standing there on her front porch weeping as I asked her if she would like to be saved, and she said she would. I prayed with her and she made her peace with God on her front porch down an old dirt road in the mountains.

God finds people in the mountains, in remote places and gives them His riches from glory. He finds them in their lost condition and makes them fellow citizens of His kingdom. He is a merciful God and He cares for all people.

Another dear, sweet lady that faithfully attended our church asked me if I would call on her son who was sixty years old and had a very serious drinking problem. I spoke to a man who knew the son and he warned me that I shouldn't go to his place unless I wanted to get shot. A few days later the mother called me and said he was on a drunken binge, his wife had left him and he had been in the house all week. She was worried so I went to her house and she got in the car and took me to his home. Her plan was that she would go in and see if he would see me. I waited in the car until she waved to me and I went in. He was flat on his back in the bed so I stood by the side of his bed. Soon his mother brought me a little cane woven stool to sit on.

I introduced myself and he started crying and asked me, "What makes me do this?" I told him that he needed God's help in his life, and that he must first repent and make peace with God. He agreed and I prayed with him and he gave his heart to the Lord. His wife came in the door about that time and he told her to write me a check for one hundred dollars. I thanked him and headed for home. The next day his mother called me and she said she believed he got the victory because he had been singing all day, "At the cross, at the cross, where I first saw the light." Mom was very happy. That Sunday I showed the man who had told me the guy might shoot me the check, and when he saw it he said he didn't believe his eyes.

When God enters a man's heart his whole world is changed. His desires are changed. He becomes a new creature in Christ Jesus. God has been known to tame the vilest of sinners and make them as gentle as a little puppy. God takes the devil out and puts the glory in. It's a wonderful thing to be set free. Praise His Holy Name Forever!

A Family in Need

As I began exploring the community and calling in many homes I discovered a low income housing area in Campton where there were many apartments. I began knocking on doors and meeting several new families. Many of them would ride the church van each Sunday which helped our attendance much. I remember knocking on one door and an elderly lady opened the door just a crack to see who was there. I introduced myself and invited her to come to our church. She said, "Oh no, I couldn't do that. I have an invalid husband and a twenty one year old son that had a stroke from using drugs and I just can't leave them. I would love to go but I must care for my husband and my son."

I asked her if I could come in and pray for them. This pleased her and she invited me in. I had prayer with both of them and visited with them for a while. I placed their names and address in my call book and began calling on them on a regular basis. I knew that I had found a family who was in need for someone to care and help them.

That was my desire from day one as a minister. I thought it was an impossible situation as far as getting them to come to church, but God showed me early that there is much more to the ministry than getting people in church to boost attendance numbers. So, I continued calling on them on a regular basis. We became friends and I soon found out that Mr. Tibbs was a retired Mountain preacher. We shared many things as we had many things in common.

Mrs. Tibbs also began riding the church van every Sunday to church, and soon her husband got well enough to come as well. Later the son and his wife also came. I never gave it a thought that they would ever be in our church, but God who is the master of impossibilities changed their situation.

Fran and I began working with the son and his wife and we saw both of them give their hearts to Jesus. The wife was saved at a Camp Meeting on the campus at Mt. Carmel. I'll never forget as they gave the alter call she literally ran to the altar weeping out loud as she went. God met her need that night. It made Fran and me very happy as we realized God had moved on the scene and met the needs of a very needy family. Nothing is ever too hard for God because He breaks the chains that Satan has bound people with and sets them free. If the Son shall make you free; you shall be free indeed.

A Blind Man

After a few months at our church, someone suggested that we start an outreach ministry. Our plan was to tape my messages and take them to shut-ins and leave the tape player for them to listen to at their own private time. We began immediately to search for likely people.

The first person I located was a blind man. His home had two rooms built out of rough lumber from the sawmill and was about three miles out in the mountains. His home was like an outbuilding and he had nailed cardboard over the cracks between the boards to keep out the cold air. I went inside and he was seated on a truck seat which was his couch. There was a board on two blocks which was where his guests sat. Fran has often referred to this situation in telling folks how I took her way out in the mountains and sat her on a board for two hours in an old shack while I called upon a blind man.

He was a Christian and he was hungry for spiritual food. He seemed very eager to receive the tape player and a couple of messages. We instructed him to count the buttons so he could start it by himself and we left it with him. I would go back and visit him several times and have prayer with him. He would always thank me for coming by and visiting and invite me back.

We found several other shut-ins to advance our ministry and to share the gospel with that God so richly gave us. I believe when men put forth an effort seasoned with love in the name of Jesus it will bear fruit. All that sows the good seed will reap a harvest in Heaven one day. *Seek ye therefore treasures in Heaven where neither moth nor rust can corrupt, nor thieves can break through and steal.*

Grandma and the Kids

The work was sometimes tiring but every effort seemed to end in blessing. We were always sure that God walked with us everywhere we went.

Very few people drove to church and we had to haul our entire congregation from three routes out in the mountains. Some days Fran would drive our car and run one of the routes which helped a lot. There was an elderly lady who lived down a steep dirt road in a mountain holler. It would have been hard to drive the van down the steep grade so she would walk her grandchildren to the top of her lane and I would pick them up every Sunday.

One Sunday it was raining and as I approached her lane I thought surely she wouldn't be there on such a rainy day, but amazingly, she was there with her three grandchildren waiting for me to pick them up. I told her that I didn't expect to see them on such a bad morning and she replied by telling me that for many years she walked three miles over the mountain to attend night services as well. She would carry a baby in one arm, a lantern in the other and had two little ones running along behind.

Several Sunday's I would see her and the children patiently waiting for the church van standing in the rain or the snow. It always made a warm flow surge through my heart as she witnessed to me and to all her neighbors how she felt about going to church. After all she did and her faithfulness Sunday after Sunday, I didn't mind when her wild mountain boys would crawl under the seats and startle the old folks, or leave service to our outdoor toilet and end up playing in the creek getting muddy and wet. They were learning about Jesus little by little and that was enough for me. *Train up a child in the way he should go, And when he is old he will not depart from it.*

Several years later my wife and I visited that old church as guest speakers at their Homecoming service. It thrilled our hearts as we saw some of the children we pastored still attending church, and some were now carrying little babies in their arms. It reminded me once again that the devil doesn't tear down everything that God has established. God's establishments and foundations are forever and no force including the devil can remove them. When God holds His children in the cleft of the rock and covers them with His great hand, they are safe in His keeping. *If God be for us who can be against us? Greater is He that is in me than He that is in the world.*

A Man Possessed

I continued calling on people and met a family in an apartment complex. The mother was suffering from cancer, and had gotten an eye removed she was in very poor health. As I sat and visited with her I could hear sounds of a man crying in the bedroom. She told me that sometimes he cried all night and kept her awake. She was very bitter and blamed her son for her weakness. I encouraged her to pray and to be careful of allowing the devil to cause her to become bitter inside. She agreed it was a need in her life and that she would pray about it. We had prayer and I headed for home.

A few days later very early in the morning she called me and said her son had cried all night and he wanted to be saved. I hurried to town and found him sitting in a lawn chair in front of their apartment on a narrow strip of lawn between the sidewalk and street. He was crying.

I thought about the man in the Bible who was possessed by demons who lived among the tombs who no man could tame, but when Jesus set him free he was a sane and gentle man. By faith I believed this man could be delivered and set free as well. I stood beside him as he wept and I ask him if he would like to be saved and he said yes. I asked him to kneel down by his chair and he kneeled down in the wet grass right beside the street. We prayed and I believe Jesus set him free. When he got up his knees were all wet from the heavy dew but he didn't even notice. I believe a man possessed by a demon was set free that early morning in the mountains of Eastern Kentucky. Praise His Holy name!

The Junk Yard Children

Within a mile of our Church there was a junk yard that covered about a five acre field. In the edge of that junk yard was a house trailer sitting in the mud. There wasn't even any grass in the yard where the children played. I knocked on the door and a lady yelled, "Come in," so I walked into her trailer and introduced myself. It was December and she was sitting in a rocking chair with an invalid baby lying on her lap.

I talked with her and she told me that she had seven children. I asked her if they could come to church if I would pick them up and she agreed. It was Christmas time and I noticed she had taken a white pine limb and stuck it in a bucket of ashes to serve as their Christmas tree. There weren't any gifts to be seen either. I had prayer with her and prayed especially for her baby and went home.

I told my three children about seven little children who had no Christmas gifts under their tree. They weren't going to let that happen so they had a plan. We had moved all their toys they had gotten for years so they decided they didn't need them anymore. They carefully wrapped them in Christmas wrapping and had gifts for every child. That Christmas those needy children had Christmas and we had joy in our hearts as we watched our children give so unselfishly out of love. When love is given it grows and those children came every Sunday while I was their pastor. Today my prayer is that they are in church and serving the God who found them stranded in a junk yard and led them to the house of God.

Our Test of Faith

I learned a long time ago that there are bumps in the road and hills to climb, and that serving God also has some hard places to overcome. Every Christian must learn very early what it means when God's word says, "The just shall live by faith." To walk with God in this world of sin will have many battles, Satan makes sure of that. Our very survival depends upon the degree of our faith.

In the winter of 1979 the snow was twenty one inches in the yard of the parsonage and we couldn't get in or out of the road to town. We went to bed at about our usual time and I had just gotten to sleep when Fran let out a terrible scream. I flipped on the light startled out of my wits. She was having a severe seizure. I didn't know what was happening. I was in a panic wondering if it was a stroke or a heart attack. I then remembered that the road to town was impossible for our car to travel on to get to the doctor's office.

I was frantic trying to decide what to do and at the same time trying to take care of Fran. Then I remembered a man, Tom Utter, who attended our church had two Jeeps. He only lived about half a mile away and I immediately called him and he was at our door in a few minutes. He had called ahead and the doctor was waiting for us at his office. By now, Fran had stopped shaking and seemed so normal that she didn't think she needed to go to the doctor. She didn't even remember having a seizure.

The doctor examined her and could find nothing, but as we left his office he told me she could have three or four more before morning. That put me on edge, and I didn't want to stay with her by myself so I asked Tom if he would mind staying the night with us. He sensed my fears and he was so kind to sleep on our couch and spend the night.

The doctor scheduled Fran an appointment with another doctor in Lexington to conduct some tests. We had very little money and no Insurance, but we believed God would work it out some way. Before we left for Lexington Tom stopped by and handed me a blank check. He said, "We are not rich, but the wife and I don't want you and Fran to go without any money." Tears were in our eyes on our way to Lexington as we realized God had stepped in to our rescue once again.

The Church was praying, and we were praying that God would intervene, and He did. Not only could the doctors not find anything wrong, but the state of Kentucky paid the whole bill which was quite large. When I returned home I gave the blank check back to the Utters. It made me feel so good to return it. The kindness that they had shown came from a heart filled with God's love and a great load of pressure was lifted as we continued to serve God in the mountains.

The days ahead proved that I had a serious problem. I remembered what the doctor had said that Fran could have many more seizures so for several weeks I couldn't sleep. Every time she would flinch in her sleep I was on full alert. I was full of fear that she would have another seizure. I went into a deep depression and I couldn't even taste the food I tried to eat.

One evening some pastors nearby, John and Barbra Amspaugh, who had become dear friends of ours stopped by to visit. They stayed for a good while and I became drowsy and felt like I could sleep. I asked them if they would stay the night and keep an eye on Fran, and that I believed that I could finally sleep. They agreed and so I went to bed.

About an hour later John came to the door and asked me if I was asleep and I said, "No John I can't sleep a wink." I've never forgotten his words as he answered, "Robert you are going to have to trust God." I thought that I was, but down deep I knew that I wasn't or I wouldn't be suffering in this depression. I looked up to God and prayed a short prayer asking the Lord to please help me and strengthen my faith. The next day I had a full appetite and I've been eating with it ever sense.

Fran never had another seizure ever again. Those were the hardest days I ever went through, and if my faith had been what it should have been I would have never had so many sleepless nights. Fran also went through a very trying time in her life. One day she was lying on the couch during her sickness and said she wanted to see the kids. All three of our children were staying on campus and we only brought them home on the weekends.

It was fifteen miles away and it was snowing so hard you couldn't see your hand in front of your face. I told her this, but she insisted so I drove into Campton. On the way to get the children, I met up with a lady who attended our church, Lucy, and asked her if she would stay with Fran while I went to pick up the children. She agreed to go to our house and sit with her.

I made it fine until I got to the road that led to the school. When I turned onto the road the car began to slide toward an embankment above the river. It looked as if I would surely go over the embankment into the river, but God helped me to get the car under control and I went on to the school. I picked up the children and headed for home. It was still snowing very heavy.

Just about two miles up the road, we came to a steep hill with a sharp curve going up it. I looked up and saw an empty coal truck sliding toward us on my side of the road. There was a guard rail on the shoulder and I had nowhere to escape. The truck was now in a jack knife condition and the bed was coming straight at us. There was only time to say, "God help us," and He did. The driver gained control of the truck and missed us by inches. I believe God has His Angels watching over His children and He sent them to our rescue on that icy mountain curve. He protected us all the way home.

Fran enjoyed having our children home and it helped in her recovery. I remembered something Dr. Paulo once said, "You don't mind the journey when you know the road leads home." I have learned for sure that the journey with Jesus may have some pot holes, steep hills and mud roads, but when Jesus walks beside us He will help us safe on our journey. Sometimes He asks us to stand in the gap in some rough waters, and just about the time you think you are going to drown, a small voice says, "Peace be still," and then a sweet calm settles down around you. "Faith is the victory, oh glorious victory."

Our faith was discovered at a little mountain Church in a blessed mountain valley. This fact motivates Fran and me as we continue the call God has placed on our life. We too thank God for the trials and infirmities that Paul spoke of because it truly was in the middle of the trial that God's hand was revealed and because of Him we left every trial behind us in victory. When the battles come, stand firm and face them. See the hand of God revealed as you win every one.

Our ministry in the mountains of Eastern Kentucky proved to be the very fountain of our faith as we witnessed God's hand time and time again. Our sweetest memories go back to that little one room church standing at the edge of a mountain valley called the Bear Pen Community Church. I can still hear the echo of its bell ringing across the holler on a snowy Sunday morning. It seems like only yesterday when Fran, the children, and I sat on the second seat from the front and sang from the bottom of our hearts, "I'll go where you want me to go dear Lord, over mountain, or plain, or sea. I'll say what you want me to say dear Lord; I'll be what you want me to be."

PART THREE

INSPIRATIONAL MESSAGES
OF
FAITH AND HOPE

CHAPTER FOUR
Leaving the Mountains

AFTER SPENDING TWO AND one half years in the Bible School it became necessary for us to move back to Southern Indiana in order to continue my studies for ministers in the Church Of The Nazarene. We began making plans and packing. While we were packing, two different men dropped by and asked me if we would stay if they started coming to church. It made our decision much harder, but we knew the time had come as God was leading us to another work in His harvest field. We said our goodbyes and with a heavy heart we were on our way. It gave me a lonely feeling to leave our dear friends behind.

God went before us and opened doors immediately for us to continue in the ministry at New Harmony, Indiana. We went for a trial sermon and I was accepted as their Pastor. It was a beautiful church with stained glass windows and a very sweet church family who Fran and I fell in love with. The parsonage also was modern and very comfortable. We praised God for giving us a nice home and a place to fulfill our calling.

The church grew in numbers almost immediately we felt blessed and honored as God begin to work in our midst. The church was in debt so they could only pay me thirty dollars a week salary, and the District sent an additional thirty dollars a week which gave us sixty dollars a week. We knew that wouldn't pay the bills and buy groceries, so Fran begin to babysit and I begin looking for work as well.

I found a nice Blackberry patch a few miles from town and I took orders for berries and sold them for five dollars a gallon. That summer I picked fifty gallons of berries and sold them without any trouble. It was nicer to pick in Indiana as compared to mountains in Kentucky filled with rattlesnakes. One of the patches I found in the mountains was way down in a ravine where the weeds were as high as my head. I would smash down the weeds to make a nice wide path so I might see the snakes.

I didn't have to worry too much about snakes in Indiana though except for a few poisonous Copperheads in the area. It was sometimes hard and even dangerous, but God has Guardian Angels to look after His children. The Bible says, "His Angels are encamped round about us." I've found that to be very true.

One day a friend in the Church said if I would go out into the sands I could buy watermelons and cantaloupes wholesale and sell them for a profit. So, I found a melon farmer and spoke to him about buying melons. He told me I hit him at just the right time, and that he was overloaded that day. He asked me twenty cents each for the cantaloupes in a nearby wagon. I think he was just being kind to me and gave me a good deal. I only had a Dodge car so I had to put them in the trunk. I put as many as I could in the trunk and took off. I went door to door and sold them all for a dollar a piece. I made about one hundred dollars in about four hours of peddling door to door.

I went back almost every day and soon I purchased a 72 Chevy pick-up and loaded it full. The farmer told me of a shady spot by the side of highway 66 where I might do well and not have to go door to door. I found the spot and it turned out to be a permanent spot for twenty five years.

Most of the Churches I pastored were small and were in reasonable distance of my selling spot near Wadesville, Indiana. I would drive to the melon fields, load up until the bumper was about to drag the ground, and drive to my spot. I made friends with many people who would stop on a regular basis for many years. It became a supplement income for us and allowed us at the same time to continue working in the smaller churches. A great man said to me one day, "Where there is a will, there is ten ways." I have never forgotten his words when I face a hard place.

Our ministry at New Harmony had several victories as God led. One year we had forty four people in attendance, most were already saved, but several were for the first time in their life. We praised God who does all things well.

After two years I finished my studies and I was ordained. I'll never forget that day because I had prayed that God would give me something spiritual to put into my testimony when I gave my report. The day I was to be ordained we were running late and that was one day I didn't want to be late. We started for Evansville, Indiana and we remembered we forgot something so we turned around and went back to the church.

When we pulled into the driveway we noticed a young man on a bicycle, he was about twenty years old. I asked him if I could help him and he said he wanted to be saved. I thought of how we didn't have time, but then I realized this was more important than being ordained. So, we took him into the church and at the altar and he gave his heart to Jesus. God gave me something very special to tell in my testimony. On the day I was ordained, I knelt with a young man at an altar of prayer. Incidentally, I was on time at my ordination and it was a very special day in my life.

We enjoyed the ministry in New Harmony for six years where we made many new friends in the area that we still make contact with occasionally. We never traveled a single mile in the work of the Lord that we can't look back and find great blessings in. The narrow way sometimes is toilsome and stressful, but Jesus never leaves us in the desert without giving us a fresh drink of water, and strength to go on. The joy that Jesus put within is a spring of refreshing water that I have learned to draw from often.

The world and all of its forces can't take away what God has put in my soul. He is a living presence in every man's life that will put their trust in Him. It's not what we are going through that matters but it's who we're going through it with that makes the difference. I love the old song *If Jesus Goes with me I'll Go Anywhere.* There is no journey to impossible for our Lord because He has already conquered them all when He died on the cross, and rose from the grave. When our faith takes hold of the hand of Jesus the dark path ahead of us becomes lighted and visible for every step we take.

One day while sitting in a lawn chair by the side of the highway selling melons a man walked up to me and asked if I was a preacher. I told him I was, and then he said he was an alcoholic and needed help. I asked him if he would like for me to pray for him, and he said he would. I had him to kneel down by an old log there in the woods and he gave his heart to the Lord. He left and I never saw him again, but one day in glory I hope to see him once again. He was a man in desperate need and Jesus met his need that day by an old log in the woods. You don't have to have a velvet lined altar and a cushion lined knee bench to find Jesus. Our Lord will come to you wherever you are, and meet your need.

Our journey which started in the mountains of Eastern Kentucky has led us to many paths where God has used Fran and me many times. We both count it a joy to be counted worthy to serve in God's great vineyard. We don't have great numbers of souls that we have won for Jesus, but we have always believed that little is much if God is in it. To God be the glory!

Our Children

Our two daughters are both pastors' wives, and our son a principal in a grade school, and he also serves in his church as Sunday School Superintendant and teacher. We praise God for Christian children. Fran and I have nine grandchildren and five great grandchildren. God truly has blessed us in many ways. You'll never come up short serving God.

I, along with Fran's help, still serve as supply pastor in Southern Indiana where we have been for the past eleven years. We plan to stay there during our retirement years as God leads. The little farm that we sold to go into the ministry is only five miles up the road from where we have built our retirement home.

Many years ago we bought one hundred and forty acres on a contract and it was mostly wooded. Across the years I sold timber off the property to keep us going and meet the payments. We never realized how God worked it out to where we could pastor in very small churches and still have money to live on, until we look back and see how he planned the whole way.

Before we retired, Fran and I talked about retirement, and we didn't see how we were going to work it out with our debt of $110,000. The road ahead looked rough for our income and we didn't know how we could make it. But, God has always made a way for his children and something unexpected happened.

A man who represented a large company knocked on our door and said they were interested in buying our ground. They made us an offer of $4,000 an acre for one hundred and ten acres. We agreed that we wouldn't need all that ground where we were going, so we met and closed the deal. They wrote us a check for $441,000. We didn't know whether to cry or shout. We had never seen so much money in all our lives and we both knew that once again God had made a way when it seemed there was none. We praise Him with all our hearts.

As soon as we got the money we paid off all our debts, bought a new car, and put the rest in a safe investment. I never dreamed that the little farm where we raised our children, and gave it up to go into the ministry, would pay with such dividends of blessings. Fran and I are able to help others now in a way that we never could before. We praise God for victory in Jesus.

As I look back so many years ago, I remember our first trip to the mountains in Eastern Kentucky where we were rooted and grounded in faith. I see the Godly people who extended a helping hand by their words of wisdom and their faith in God. I will always have a heart full of gratitude and love for a holy people who serve God with their mind, soul, and body. When God calls I say to all, surrender to his will by saying, "Here am I Lord, I'm not much but I give you my life, and use me as thou will." You'll never be sorry for giving of your best to the Master.

The ministry led us to many events and blessings, and this book would not be complete without the heart of the gospel included that the Spirit has taught me these many years. These next chapters will include messages that I feel give strength to the soul and light to any path as the Spirit leads.

CHAPTER FIVE
God's Little People

GOD HAS A PLACE in His great army of followers for little people who have no particular skills or abilities. In the midst of those who are mighty and thunder from the pulpits of the gospel, and those mighty in spiritual application and expression of many gifts, God still has a place for those who seem inefficient and weak. Those who have feel they have no special gifts or abilities, or never receive any rewards or special tribute to recognition.

These little people are the unsung heroes that serve God because of their love, and devotion to Him and His Kingdom. They look for no earthly rewards and feel even undeserving of such rewards. They walk the narrow way by choice and follow the markings and footprints of Jesus. He instructs and they hear and obey. Their ambition is not a building program or a social function to enrich numbers in attendance, but to fill their space where Jesus has placed them and to see men saved.

The salvation of souls is their goal. They often wonder why people don't love God as much as they do. To worship is all the reason they need to go to church. They disagree with those who sweeten up peoples' desires to be in church by using all sorts of social gimmicks and entertainment. They believe that when people come only when certain conditions are met, they are failing true worship, and God won't buy it. They believe socialism is as big an error as emotionalism and all who go to church for those reasons or promote the same become man's business and not God's business.

On judgment day it's not going to be everyone that attended church that has a ticket to heaven, but it will be those who have been transformed by the blood of Jesus and possess an unconditional love to worship God. Gods little people face unfavorable conditions and hard places but meet them with a determined will to go on and to stand and face the battle Satan has set to hinder God's will. When love reins we face the rain along with the sunshine with joy and understanding.

No worldly pleasure or attraction can change their depth of love for God, for they know Satan places them there to distract and destroy their relationship with Him. Their appetite for the world no longer controls their life because Jesus broke the chains and set them free and gave them peace that the world could never give. They know God is a God of equality and fairness. They know that paupers will stand with kings in God's kingdom of heaven and that Earth's little people will stand just as tall as the next one in heaven. In heaven the ground is level.

They know that God loves all people. People that live on the streets without homes, people that live in fear and hunger driven about like herds of cattle. They know that God's love reaches into the darkest places on the face of the earth to rescue those that are lost and without hope, and gives them purpose and meaning in their lives. They are God's little people that can walk with their head up in the rain and in the storms of life because they have met the Master of life's storms and have heard the words of Jesus, "Peace be still."

I remember my Godly Mother who was one of God's little people. She carried a burden for the lost and always watched for an opportunity to lead someone to Christ. One day Mother and Dad were driving near their home, when they passed by a wooded area. Since it was summer their windows were down in the car and they heard a cry for help. Mother had Dad stop the car and told him to go see who it was. Dad was reluctant so Mother climbed up the bank and over a fence out into the woods. There she found a man that had been shot in the stomach with a shotgun by a trespasser. The man was dying from loss of blood.

Mother's first words were "Are you a Christian?" The man answered that he wasn't. Mother then asked him if he would like her to pray for him, he said yes I would. Shortly after, as they loaded him into an ambulance, he reached out his hand to Mother and told her thank you and that he felt like he had been helped. He died on the way to the hospital.

Mother, one of God's little people, never got a write up in the paper, nor did she want one. Her reward was to give to others what Jesus had given to her. Every night as I was growing up I would hear my mother praying out loud in the darkness of our home. I would snuggle up in my bed and feel safe because Mother asked God to protect us through the dark night, and I believed that He would. She was one of God's little people who believed in God's love and care, and we children knew God had heard our mother pray and He would take care of us

When I was a child, we lived in a log house by the highway with a large front lawn filled with maple trees. One of our neighbors would mow the roadside with a team of horses by a pull type mower. He only had one arm, and we children called him One Arm Charlie. We would run and wave as he passed by and when he returned he would bring us a couple pints of ice cream. Mom would divide the ice cream for each of us. He was a kind man and we loved him.

It didn't surprise me when we went to camp meeting and saw One Arm Charlie and his wife there every night. He was another one of God's little people from the good old days who counted it a joy to give kindness to others. The love of Jesus is always evident in God's little people and they give of themselves for the good of others. They are never forgotten by those whose lives they have touched.

I believe when love and kindness are given it grows, and it never fails to be rewarded. The bible says, "Cast your bread upon the waters and after many days it will return unto you again," also, "whatsoever a man sows, that shall he also reap." Good will follow good, love will follow love and peace will follow peace. A sweet harvest will come to all of God's little people who give for the good of others one day in glory.S

Earthly paths hold the footprints of God's little people and the seed they have sown is reproduced in those they have touched. The world owes a great debt to those we call God's little people.

From Genesis verse one to the last verse of Revelations there is a long, narrow and winding road that crosses deserts, mountains and valleys. There are floods, fires and strong winds. There are those who war against God's divine plan and set their armies in the middle of the road to attract God's band of followers. But, the mighty arm of God parts the sea of armies, quenches the heat and fire of the furnaces, locks up the jaws of the lions, breaks the keepers off prison doors and sends a beacon of light. He illuminates and drives back the often dark nights so that His winding road can be seen no matter how dark the day may seem.

When thunder roars and the lightning flashes a rainbow appears in the dark clouds. As the band of followers sometimes tremble and fear grips hold of them, a still small voice calls to them, "Fear not for I am with thee even unto the end of the world." As the enemy sets the battle before them God would call to them. Deuteronomy 31:6 *Be strong and of good courage, fear not nor be afraid of them. Fear the Lord thy God, He it is that doth go with thee, He will not fail thee nor forsake thee.*

This is now 2010 and the straight and narrow road has won every battle that was ever set against it all these years. It may have some wounded soldiers with scars from many battles, and many that have been slain in the way, but when one falls, another takes their place. They continue the journey with their eyes set on the city of God where the battles will cease forever. They have learned that the resistance in their path is man's artillery, only the arm of flesh, and they have witnessed Angels encamped around them driving back those evil forces always coming to their rescue. They have the master of the battle on their team. They live in victory because their trust is in Jesus who is the victor.

They are God's Little People

My wife and I give tribute to all who stand tall for Jesus in love and sacrifice. Those who have went on to be with Jesus and left us a call to follow in their same love. Each time I walk into a church, I am reminded of the privilege I have to use such establishment as God's house because people before me fought the battles, paid the bills, and kept the lower lights burning. We owe a great debt to those who have gone on to Glory who gave of themselves for the good of others, and who left behind a refuge and a shelter for future generations to enjoy.

Truly we are treading where the saints of God have trod. May we maintain the church and obey God as those faithful children of the past did for us. May the next generation inherit a refuge and shelter where praise can't be interrupted or delayed. Let us leave tracks behind us that follow the path of righteousness that leads to God.

I believe that the way we attend church today will determine how serious onlookers will regard the importance of worshiping God in the future. If we attend church today as if it is optional it will plant the seed that grows the roots of neglect which would be a slow death to the house of worship. May we let the faithfulness of those of the past inspire us to set the same example by maintaining God's house on earth in this day of ungodly men.

Today on the news they reported that they changed the name from 'Christmas Parade' to 'Holiday Parade' in a city in Oklahoma. The Mayor of the city who had ridden a horse in the parade for the past thirty years, refused to ride again until they changed it back to 'Christmas Parade.'

Here is an example of how we should take our stand and when we do people will notice. The fight for right requires good soldiers who are willing to stand before the world and resist the devil and all his supporters. When we do, the world will notice our unbending faith in the living God. The battle is won when men and women refuse to retreat and stand firm against the vast numbers of ungodly multitudes who wish to remove the name of Jesus from our society. This makes me think of the old song, *Take the Name of Jesus with You.*

CHAPTER SIX
Heart Thoughts

I'VE NOTICED THAT IN sin the things we hold on to are the things we lose. But, in salvation, the things we deny are the things that we keep forever, and what we thought we didn't want turn out to be our greatest blessings.

Satan has attractive establishments where at the entrance appears bright and beautiful, but after you walk into his world you become like the prodigal son who learned the hard lesson. The world is not your friend and will not assist you in your ruin and despair. God *is* a true friend who comes to you in your ruin. He nourishes you with love and care and helps you get back on your feet. God lifts you out of the heartbreaks and pain that Satan led you into with his false fronts of beauty and joy. He sets a trap with things that looks and taste good, but at the end of that fruit is bondage, heartbreak, and despair.

The prodigal son learned this lesson the hard way. He ended up alone, all his resources were gone, and those who pretended to be his friends now had no use for him. It was at this point that he remembered how much better he had it under his father's shelter and care that he had left behind. He realized that the greener grass that he saw on the other side of the fence and ran to turned out to be desert and dry land.

He remembered real love, real shelter, and real peace in his father's care. He remembered the warmth and togetherness of his family and friends. And so, he returned with a greater understanding. As he journeyed back, the closer he got to home, the brighter the way became. The lesson that he learned we should all learn: Home under our Father's care is where the grass is always greener than you may think.

God has a lush, green pasture where he feeds and nourishes his sheep, and where he protects them from dangers that often come. He leads them through the darkness and storms of life. He never leaves them alone or unattended. He is our heavenly father who is committed to the care and well being of his children. He is the good shepherd. God never takes from, but he gives daily to each of us all the issues of life. Satan rapes your soul of joy, happiness, friends and family contentment. He influences divorce, family division, and heartbreak. The world doesn't have the treasures that our heavenly home holds for us in love.

As for me, I'm content down on the farm with its struggles and hard places. Real happiness is a whole lot closer than most people realize. Look closely around you and see what God has given you. Hold to it as you hold to his hand. Don't take hold of that extended hand of the devil, who wants to lead you into despair and heartbreak. Look more closely around you and see the blessings God has already given you, and will continue giving you.

Don't be deceived as Satan points out all the things you don't have and all the things you could have, but look at the blessings you do have in walking with God. Let us be grateful for life's little moments and feast on them every day, for they are enlarged in love, and become the very fuel for happiness and joy.

How our hearts are warmed by the memories of our endurance outlives obstacles and hard trials. Our hearts are warmed because we remember it was Jesus who nourished us and led us across the deep valleys and also the high mountains. The lord is my strength and shield. My heart trusts in Him and I am helped, every time, every place, and in every situation. Let love abound that God has given to you in good measure. Let it abound to your wife, to your husband, to your children, to your friends and to all around you.

Love never fails. Love will be the stone that kills the giants of separation every time and bring two hearts back together. When love is real, and God is real to us, life becomes an adventure of joy with positive expectation. It is then that we walk with assurance and trust, and are even eager to go on and face the next battle. Let each of us inventory and see if what we have is not a grander gift than what we thought we didn't have. Rebuke the devil who attempts to stir us away from the lush, green grass that grows by the running stream of living water that with it, we will never hunger or thirst again. We are safe in the arms of God.

I hope these words seasoned by the Holy Spirit will encourage your heart, and help to guide you up the winding, narrow path of life that Jesus has cleared. He is the captain of our salvation, and the captain marks the true way to eternal life. As I have said many times before, when Jesus died on the cross He won every battle that we will ever face. Never forget the battle has already been won on the cross of redemption.

CHAPTER SEVEN
Walking With a Friend

(Pro. 18:24) *And there is a friend that sticks closer than a brother.*

When you journey with a friend the journey is pleasant. It's a lonely and dark journey when you walk alone. The only sound you can hear is your own footsteps on a dark and lonely street, but when you hear the footsteps of a friend walking beside you the night is less dark and a sense of courage takes hold. Never forget; Jesus will walk with you down the dark streets of your journey. You are never alone because Jesus is a true friend.

I remember when I was a small boy and Dad took me coon hunting with him. Our dog picked up a coon trail and took out across the woods. Dad instructed me to wait by a tree until he returned. Dad had our only lantern which he took with him on the chase. It was very dark and I became afraid while waiting. Soon I saw a tall shadow coming toward me crashing through the brush. It was Dad. The fear left and then I felt safe with him close by. I think that night long ago I learned what it means to be alone in a dark world and I learned the safe feeling with a strong man beside me.

Jesus is the strongest of all, and when He walks with us we face life and all of its dark days bravely and with courage because we know He will not fail us. Jesus gives strength to the weak, and hope to the discouraged. He gives light to all who walk in darkness, and lifts those who are sinking in the sands of sin and places their feet on the solid rock. You can believe that He cares for you and me, and He knows our dangers ahead that will harm us.

(John 10:3) *He calls his own sheep by name, and leads them out.*

I'll say it again, when you walk the journey with a friend, the journey is a pleasant one and you can be sure JESUS IS THAT FRIEND THAT STICKETH CLOSER THAN A BROTHER.

We notice when Jesus walked among men He had a vision that searched for the one lost sheep. His eyes would scan the hills and the valleys searching for the sheep that was hurting, the sheep that Satan deceived and led astray. His eyes would see the cripple, or the blind man, the hungry and the thirsty, and He helped them. Jesus looked for those in need, those that were lost and led them to safety. Jesus breaks the chains of Satan that has men bound and sets them free.

Jesus walks through the dark valleys searching for those who have lost their way and He leads them back on course, on the road that leads to glory. Jesus furnishes the grace to overcome and to endure, but we must come to the fountain and drink where the grace is given. You'll never be cured of the sickness of helplessness until you drink at the fountain of Jesus, where strength and courage is given. You have to go to the fountain where the glory flows out before you can drink the living water, and that's enough to make a quite man shout!

Running through life alone and on your own steam will leave you in a dark and lonely valley, but putting your hand in the hand of Jesus will give you a friend that will stand by you when all others flee. Jesus has a sure grip and He won't let go when the going gets rough because His love for you is inseparable. Nothing can separate us from the love of God. Who wouldn't want a friend like Jesus? He is a true friend, a safe friend, an unconditional friend. He offers His friendship to all and He accepts us where we are to come to Him. He says, "Call and I will answer, seek and ye shall find, knock and it shall be opened unto you."

There is a friend that sticks closer than a brother. Praise His Holy Name!

Satan pretends to be your friend, but we have seen the results of those he has deceived and led astray. He rapes your soul of joy, happiness, and friends. He takes away family togetherness, and he robs you of the things that really count. He influences divorce and family division. He doesn't want you to be happy. Satan thrives on destroying family relations that bring unrest in the home. He is a rascal and there is no good in him.

We must remember that when Jesus died on the cross He defeated the devil forever. Our lord is the victor and His grace is sufficient. There is enough power in one drop of His blood to put the devil and all of his demons on the run forever. The devil is, and will forever be, a defeated foe because of Jesus who died on an old rugged cross. Jesus will never leave you or forsake you. Oh what a Savior, Oh what a friend, His name is Jesus.

CHAPTER EIGHT

A Young Man's Journey

(Luke 15:11-13) *A certain man had two sons, and the younger of them said to his father, "Father, give me the portion of goods that falls to me." And he divided unto them his living. And not many days after the younger son gathered all together, and took his journey into a far country, and there wasted his substance with riotous living. And when he had spent all, there arose a mighty famine in the land; and he began to be in want.*

This story that Jesus gives us about the prodigal son could be a true account of many young men and women in our world today. The world attracted him and he went out into sin wasting away his life, money and all that he had. Then when all his resources were gone, he looked around where he had ended up and he realized he had made a terrible mistake. His money was gone, the friends he thought he had were gone, and he suddenly realized how alone he was in this big world. Then he remembered the love and care that he had left behind and ran back to his father and family.

I have found that the home where I was raised had the greenest grass on earth where Mother and Dad loved and cared for me. I would love to run barefoot through that yard and feel the green grass under my bare feet once again. I would love to hear Mother's voice calling me to supper once again, and see the sunset lighting up the sky over the old barn roof.

Dad and Mother had restrictions at home that we children had to follow to the letter. To disobey them would mean we a punishment. Dad worked long hours so most of the time Mom taught and corrected us children when we broke the rules or disobeyed them. Mother's values were constructed from a Holiness church and biblical preaching, so the rules that Mom and Dad wrote on our conscience were scriptural and right.

I can remember when I would break one of the *Thou shall not*'s and no one knew about it, an awful guilt would set in, and at night before I would go to sleep, I would pray and ask God to forgive me. Then the guilt would go away. We were taught about Heaven and Hell at a very young age, and that sin would take us to that awful place of torment. Saying bad words, smoking, drinking, gambling, and going to picture shows was not allowed. My early years of discipline were right and they made me a better person in the long run. I am glad that Mother and Dad were so firm in their values.

I was like the prodigal son as a young man. I thought all the fun was out in the world away from Mom, Dad and home so I left those things to begin my journey. As soon as I was sixteen, I quit school got me a job and bought an automobile. I even had my own apartment. I was free at last to do as I pleased, and so I did. I wanted to see what this big world had to offer me and I wanted to do all the things that I was not allowed to do while I was at home.

I started with the movie theater. There were several in the city where I lived so some days I would take in three different theaters. The hungering for the things of the world overwhelmed me and I drifted out into sin. Like the prodigal son, I went on an adventure to taste of the forbidden fruits that I had never tasted. Although I enjoyed myself, I found that guilt never left my soul as I traveled my journey of sin and worldly pleasures. That guilt followed me no matter where I went or what I did. Today my experience reminds me of a scripture. *Train up a child in the way he should go and when he is old it will not depart from him.* I found this to be true. I was because of the Christian values Mother and Dad taught me as I grew up that I felt that guilt. It was the very thing that later in life led me to God and to salvation, and then into the ministry of Jesus Christ.

I have preached the blessed gospel for many years and the joy that I thought I was missing at home is the very joy that was there all the time. Like the prodigal son, my adventure in the world was only an empty and dry journey that didn't satisfy and only left me in want. I thank God for the Godly heritage that reached into my soul and called me back home where life was sweet.

I believe when parents sow the seed of the rights and wrongs of Christian life and the consequences of sin in their children at a young age, it will one day bear fruit. Doing this will result in your wayward sons and your daughters will find their way back to God and salvation. Heaven holds countless numbers of disobedient children that found their way back home and back to God because of Godly parents who taught them about Heaven, hell and Jesus while they were growing up. There will be shouts of victory as the tears of hurt flow away while walking the streets of Glory hand in hand.

I don't wish to describe the other side of the spectrum. The side of those who knew not about Jesus because their parents lived a life of sin before their children, those who failed to attend church or train them in the way of salvation and Holiness. The worst child abuse on earth is to fail to take children to church and teach them about salvation, and about God. They need to know the results of sin at an early age, and they need to be held back from running with the worldly crowd. When the lines have been cut and they are turned loose to run as they will, your heart will be broken as the world takes them in and destroys their life.

Across the years in my ministry, I have heard the testimony of a weeping mother many times who regretted not getting saved while her children were growing up, and that maybe they would have turned out better if she had. I've visited their children in jail, and I've preached their funerals where Satan took into eternity without God. I've visited them in hospitals from drug overdose and auto wrecks from drunk driving. I've watched their children grow up, get married and end up brokenhearted with a divorce and broken home.

There is a better way. It is the way of the cross where victory is found and happiness blossoms in the home and peace flows like a river. Remember, Jesus said, "Peace, be still," and there was a great calm. I remember when the children of Israel were set free from bondage the first thing they did was rebuild their altar of worship. The Bible says, "Their weeping was as loud as their shouts of victory." God's way is the best way to happiness and a fulfilling, complete life. *Train up a child in the way he should go and when he is old he will not depart from it.*

CHAPTER NINE
Creating Our Own Clouds

(Matthew 7:1-2) *Judge not, that ye be not judged. For with what judgment ye judge, ye shall be judged, and with what measure ye mete, it shall be measured to you again. And why behold thou the mote that is in thy brother's eye, but consider not the beam that is in your own eye? Or how wilt thou say to thy brother, let me pull the mote out of your eye; and, behold, a beam is in your own eye. Thou hypocrite, first cast out the beam out of your own eye; and then shall thou see clearly to cast out the mote out of thy brothers eye.*

Sometimes we can't see the glow of God's glory in others because of the dark clouds we place before them by our judgment. If our view of that person is darkened because of a lack of confidence, their testimony will fall flat before you and in turn you may miss a great blessing. When God is using a person to glorify His name, and we can only see that person as a questionable Christian because of things they do that we feel is wrong, then we are judging that person. Even worse than that, we are placing a dark cloud between our vision and God's glorious glow. Simply, we miss the glory by our own blindness, and we build our own cloudy skies by our judging of others.

God uses he who will glorify His name, and we should receive the glory rather than to criticize the person God is using. I remember a very special service in our church. Someone requested the song *I Surrender All*, and as we begin singing softly, a certain lady stood to her feet signifying her full surrender to God. During the second verse, others stood to their feet, and one by one everyone in the church was standing. The Spirit overwhelmed us and all knew that God's Spirit had visited each of us with a heavenly presence. If others had felt that the lady that stood first was questionable, it would have killed the service, and dark clouds of judging would have hid the glory of

God's presence. But, as each stood voluntarily, we continued singing softly, and God gave us a great blessing.

God's will must always be first in our decisions. His will is clearly revealed and easily discovered because God makes His way known to all men. All who walk in darkness make their own choice because the way of God is well lit. Surrender is the word that leads home, and self will is the word that leads farther and farther from God where the days only grow darker. When we shut people out by judging them unfit to be carriers of His light we have resisted the light and judging others is sin.

I believe God is calling His children to lend a listening ear to truth. He gives light in a thousand different ways, and uses a thousand different voices to guide our steps. In the judgment days, people look on Jesus and His disciples as the enemy. They threw them in jail, beat them, and refused to hear their words. How wrong they were as they judged them unfit to be heralds of the almighty God. Their words brought light to a self righteous and arrogant people who were walking in darkness. This blundering came simply by judging others by their narrow minded concept of righteousness, which was manmade, and not God sent. There were many who ignored the truth.

Today our world is walking in midnight darkness and doing immorality has replaced the righteousness of God. Millions walked down the dark road to ruins when God lit up a bright and clear path through His witnesses around the world. People blunder in darkness, as if they have no eyes to see or ears to hear, but then God lights the way to everlasting life and joy. Don't be guilty of building a wall of dark clouds that hide God's glory by judging others.

CHAPTER TEN
Life's Hard Places

(Psalms 28:7) *The Lord is my strength and my shield; my heart trusted in Him, and I am helped.*
(Psalms 27:1) *The Lord is my light and my salvation: Whom shall I fear? The Lord is the strength of my life; of whom shall I be afraid.*

Nothing in life that was ever accomplished, that amounted to anything, was ever accomplished without great effort, pain, and hard labor. Every good thing that was ever created always has an obstacle to overcome before accomplishment. How quickly we give up with our little blisters. The struggles of life teach us, we must lean into the wind to get up the hill when it is blowing fiercely. We must row harder when the boat is drifting with the flowing current in order to reach our destination.

Today we as Christians are in the midst of the largest storm this world has ever seen. No age was ever crueler, more selfish or more ungodly as it is today. As Christians, we are walking in the fog and dark clouds of immorality and evil men. The weight of sin surrounds each of us in every family as we toil on for Jesus. Like the song goes, "I can't feel at home in this world anymore." We must labor on and push harder as we journey on toward glory. We may have to suffer and struggle to keep on route, and at times the road may seem impossible, but the Lord gives strength to continue on. Sometimes the load we must carry is heavy and no one seems to help, but Jesus never fails to lend a strong shoulder and lighten one's load.

When it's so dark that you fear you will lose your way, a light appears before you and a heavenly presence surrounds you. Your strength is renewed as you move onward with a new surge of strength and purpose from God. David said, "The Lord is my light and my salvation, whom shall I fear." As we journey on we have a clear vision of a beautiful city that lies ahead of us, and we know that there waits a glad tomorrow.

The road can become rocky and steep, but the rocks that bruise our feet with pain only remind us of that city where they need no sun and there will never be a dark night. The pain we must endure in this life only deposits more treasures in Heaven and our hearts are conditioned with tough love for Jesus. Our trials seem like nothing when we remember the great pain Jesus took on Himself because He loved us enough to take on great suffering on the cross. Who are we to complain over such small matters?

(Psalms 28:7) *The Lord is my strength and my shield; my heart trusted in Him, and I am helped.*

CHAPTER ELEVEN
Running the Race for Jesus

IN OUR WORLD TODAY every Christian faces overwhelming odds in the battle between right and wrong as Satan attacks from every front to weaken our resistance to his suggestions. The battle is fierce and the artillery is mighty, so flesh and blood alone can never make the journey that looms before every Christian. There are many issues that we must face and overcome. Allow me to name just a few by asking these questions of grave importance:

1.) What shall we do with the approaching threats against God and against Christianity?

2.) What shall we do as evil men with terrorist intentions increase daily as they teach their young children to hate, and train them to kill innocent people?

3.) What should we do as merchants around the world watch their merchandise pile up without any buyers and fear takes hold as an economy collapses around the world in every nation?

4.) What should we do as Hollywood productions fill our television screens with nudity and every immoral act that violates the word of God without any restrictions by law?

5.) How should we prepare ourselves to face all of these oppositions that loom in our path as Christian followers of Jesus Christ?

God answers all of these questions in his holy word.
(Ephesians 6:10-11) *Finally my brethren, be strong in the Lord, and in the power of his might. Put on the whole armor of God that ye may be able to stand against the wiles of the devil.*

Let us take a good look at the armor of God and find what makes it so complete and so durable in the heat of the battle:

(Ephesians 6:14-15) *Stand therefore having your loins girt about with TRUTH and having on the breastplate of righteousness, and your feet shod with the preparation of the gospel of peace.*

(Ephesians 6:16-17) *Above all, taking the shield of FAITH, wherewith ye shall be able to quench all the fiery darts of the wicked and take the helmet of salvation, and the sword of the spirit, which is the word of God.*

This armor of God identifies the complete Christian who is fully prepared to stand for God in every battle that Satan launches against Him and His children. It is God's provision for a successful and happy life in this present evil world.

Just this past Sunday God gave me a very challenging thought that I won't forget. I hope that you too will see the picture God set before me. The reason a runner in a race runs out of wind and falls before he reaches the finish line is because he failed to condition himself before the race. This is the same reason many Christians fall or run out of wind. They failed to condition themselves by the grace of God in holiness.

Every Christian will need God's best to complete the race that we all must run. The battle is too great to win without the whole armor of God snuggly in place. Paul says in Hebrews 12:1, "Let us run with patience, the race that is set before us." As we run this race, the enemy fills our path with roadblocks and obstacles. His object is to cause us to lose the race. Every Christian will be attacked by his sudden ambushes. As Paul said, "We wrestle not against flesh and blood, but against principalities and powers, and against the rulers of darkness of this world and spiritual wickedness in high places." We are no match for these powers of darkness, and we need Christ at our side as we run this race.

Jesus illuminates the way before us, and He lights up the dark bends in the road where Satan has set his traps to ensnare and chain us to his deceptions. One of Satan's favorite obstacles is immoral permissiveness. This is a modern day sin that creeps into the churches around the world. Satan makes things in the world appear innocent and pure. By doing this, he attempts to weaken our Christian morals and values.

There is a definite spirit of permissiveness in many modern day churches that Satan has carefully slipped into this race to turn us off the route and lose the race. When permissiveness enters into the church the guilt of sin weakens in our young people as Satan paints sin a different color. By deceptive intentions Satan paints black white, but it is still black, and it is still sin. God didn't rewrite the Bible to fit a lustful and adulterous generation.

Every Christian should recognize this road block that God's word illuminates so we can see where we are running. God has never forsaken man or left him to run this race blindly, but his holy prophets have placed warning signs to avoid the quicksand of sin, and lead us on to glory. Not only does God give us revelation to identify sin, but He gives us a second wind every time the devil attacks us. With it, we can run and not be weary as we see the finish line just ahead. It is spiritual conditioning that gives us a toughness that keeps us running this blessed race all the way to the finish. When the world is at its worst moral condition in history, Christians must be at their best condition to run the distance for God. We must run the whole race to win the prize.

God's armor will meet the test with the helmet of salvation, the breastplate of righteousness, the sword of the spirit, and the shield of faith. Conditioning is a daily chore because Christians need spiritual maintenance to keep their gears running smoothly. We apply maintenance by prayer, by devotions and by faithful attendance in church. There is power in prayer and faith to use as our weapons against the enemy, and without God at our side we will never survive the many attacks by the enemy, nor will we win the race. By neglect our spiritual lives become rusty and could cause us to falter in the home stretch.

What shall we do with all these pressing issues that war against God and His Children? We condition ourselves by the grace of God that puts the wind in our sails to carry us through all the storms and turbulence that Satan so often sends our way. The sails may be torn and the ship battered and scarred from the many battles, but its flag will still be waving that reads victory when it enters into the harbor where many other ships are anchored that Captain Jesus navigated safely home. There, never will another battle be. There is much joy in the camp as all the crews celebrate with the King of Kings, and Lord of Lords. As the Bible says, "And their noise was heard afar off."

We are not the victims, but we are the victors because Jesus won every battle that we will ever face when He died on the cross. Our faith should tell us why worry if the battles have already been won. If the city of forever has already been constructed that waits for all of God's children at the end of this earthly race. Maybe the race has been rough for you and you have just about given up, or maybe you have fallen in the home stretch and your strength is almost gone. If so, look up to Jesus, and He will pick you up and place your feet back on the path. He'll give you a second wind to complete the race and reach the finish line. He never fails to pick up one of his fallen children and help them to get home where the sun shines forever and the flowers never stop blooming. It is a city of unending joy.

CHAPTER TWELVE
God's Promises

THE YEARS FRAN AND I have spent in the ministry have taught us to hold to the hand of Jesus and never let go no matter what the path may hold. God has hidden treasures just waiting for us to discover as we travel and follow his will. In this chapter, I wish to write about the promises of God. As we face all kinds of obstacles in our way that look unmovable, we must grasp hold of the promises of God.

After Noah's flood there were only eight people to face an empty world. All they had to survive with was each other. Early, as they begin their journey, God made a covenant with Noah by placing a rainbow in the clouds, and each time it appeared it would remind them of God's promises and faithfulness to lead them and protect them.

I lose my breath when after a violent storm and heavy rains a beautiful rainbow appears. I look up and take in the beauty, but I never forget to remember what the rainbow means in a spiritual sense. It is a reminder of God's unbreakable promises.

Recently, Fran and I celebrated our fiftieth wedding anniversary by taking a bus tour to Cape Cod and Niagara Falls with some friends of ours. As we were leaving the falls, our bus drove by them for one last look. As we passed by there was a rainbow that arched over the very street where we drove. There, I saw something I had never seen before. I saw the end of the rainbow within a few feet of the bus.

I thought for a moment of the story I heard as a child; there is a pot of gold at the very end of the rainbow. I yelled to my friend Bill and said, "Guess what Bill, I saw the end of the rainbow and there is no pot of gold." But, then I told him I saw an invisible treasure. All the promises of God opened up before me as I pondered in my heart the word of God. The end of the rainbow revealed to me the invisible presence of God in my heart and in my life. We all have an invisible treasure in this earthen vessel.

A great sense of trust swept over me as I viewed the beautiful rainbow, and I knew God's promises would never be broken. As I thought, a warm flow of peace flooded my soul as the Spirit spoke to my heart reminding me of the priceless treasure I have in Jesus. I just leaned back in my seat and enjoyed the thoughts that were pouring through my mind. I got a vision of the hand of God as He shelters His sheep from the dangers and hurts that often cross their path. His promises are our artillery as we face the enemy because our real power is the faith in our God to go on.

Many wonderful thoughts were flooding through mind as I listened to the spirit. I remembered God promised a savior and He sent Jesus to die for our sins. He promised the comforter, and He sent the Spirit to guide, sanctify, empower and to be a true witness. Again, I saw an invisible treasure as I viewed the rainbow. God's promises are sealed forever and we must hold onto the treasures they represent, which are His unconditional love, His providential care and the treasure of His joy that we can know and experience in our walk with Jesus. Not a pot of gold, but a treasure of far greater value.

If I tried to list all the treasures we have in Jesus I would fail. They are like the widows cruse of oil and the barrel of meal that never ran out. In sin, the heart is imprisoned and bound by Satan, the world and all of its riches cannot fill the longing of the soul. It's like a hidden treasure that you never find and the empty search goes on and on. But, the day you turn your life over to Jesus, the treasure is found that your soul sought for so long. The joy bells begin to ring, peace settles over your soul, and God sets you free, the bonds and chains have been broken. The Son has set you free from the world that you craved.

Now you have a purpose that reaches out for the good of others. Your life now is hid in Christ and you have found the joy of knowing it is more blessed to give than to receive. Now you believe that treasures are to be shared and you help others to find the treasure that you have found. By helping others find their way you will find even more treasures of blessings. A rainbow represents the promises of God and when I look at it I see much more than the beauty of its colors. I see all the blessings that God faithfully gives to all who turn to Him. I find in Jesus, treasures that neither moth nor rust can take away, nor the thieves can break through and steal. God's promises are forever true.

CHAPTER THIRTEEN
Signs of the Times

SUDDENLY OUR WORLD HAS changed in its seasonal weather patterns. We now have warnings flash across our T.V. screens telling people to take shelter. Indoor weather alarms go off in every home all hours of the night. Restful sleep is interrupted by a voice crying out to take shelter during dangerous storms. People crawl in their bathtubs, run to their basements, and in their closets trying to find a place of safety. The fact is, these violent patterns will continue because of global warming, and they will worsen according to many scientists who have been studying these conditions for years.

We are seeing what I believe is the signs of the end of the world. As the bible says, "There will be signs in the sky, and in the earth." This means visible signs will appear that we will see plainly. I believe we are seeing the formation of the beginning of sorrows, and the great tribulation period. The prophets have spoken and it will be just exactly as they have foretold. The bible says, "Be mindful of the words spoken by the prophets."

(Luke 17:26) *And as it was in the days of Noah, so shall it be also in the days of the son of man.*

(Luke 17:28) *Likewise also; as it was in the days of Lot.*

Abraham searched throughout Sodom and Gomorrah to find a few righteous men so that God would spare the cities, but he found none. The reason Abraham couldn't find any righteous people was because they had all turned away from God to commit unthinkable abominations against Him. They were pleasure mad and sinning without guilt or conviction. Their deeds were worthy of Hell's fire, and that's just what they got. They perished in their wickedness as the fire and brimstone rained down on their cities. This was a reminder that God will not tolerate sin, and the wages of sin is death.

I challenge anyone to walk through our cities anywhere in America and ask people to come to church. Their answers or remarks may involve calling you crazy, or inviting you to just take a pill and take a little trip. Walk through any city in America and you'll find Sodom and Gomorrah all over again. Jeremiah 6:15 says, "they did wicked abominations before the Lord, and were they ashamed: Nay, neither did they blush." When sin has lost its guilt we are seeing a sign that the prophets have declared would be another sign of the end of the world.

II Timothy 3: 4 calls people like the ones above, "Lover's of pleasure more than lovers of God." The way some people treat God and the church, and the way they talk in front of their children using curse words, makes me think some believe time will never run out. If they knew the truth, they would be getting their house in order. If they really believed Jesus is coming soon they would run to the altar and beg forgiveness for their sins.

This old world is running on its last leg. I believe judgment day is at our door step, and Jesus will soon appear. Where you spend eternity will depend on the decisions you make today, tomorrow may be too late. Jesus said, "You will know by the signs which will be as noticeable as the trees budding in the spring when the end is near." Tilt your ear to the eastern sky, the trumpet is about to sound.

(Matthew 24:7-8) *Nation shall rise against nation, and kingdom against kingdom: and there shall be famines, and pestilences, and earthquakes in diver's places.*

All these things are the beginnings of sorrow. I believe we are seeing the formation of the great tribulation period when weather conditions beat the earth with violent destructive forces. It will impair farmers to where they can't plant or harvest their crops. Drought and forest fires this very year have sweep across thousands of acres and destroyed hundreds of homes. Raging floods in other parts of the world have destroyed farm lands and made it impossible to raise crops. This has caused food prices to sky rocket. Weed killers and fertilizers being used today are making the food chain unhealthy and harmful. To me all of these conditions are the signs that the Bible predicted would come on the world at the end.

The prophets have already revealed a day will come to this old world that will be called the beginning of sorrows, and the great tribulation period where no flesh will be saved unless God would shorten the days, and that He would shorten those days. The end may be sooner than most people think. Jesus prophesized of a day that people would say, "blessed are the wombs that are barren."

I believe this means two things. First, population explosion, meaning more people will be on earth than can possibly be fed. At that time the cry for food will wail out around the world, but no food will be available. Even now millions are crying for food. So, tribulation will come by global starvation, drought and famine.

Secondly, "evil men will wax worse and worse." This means we will fear for our children growing up in an evil and dangerous world. Living conditions will be so unsafe mothers and fathers will hesitate to bring babies into the world. This very hour in the east mothers are wailing and crying as they embrace their dead babies in their arms who have been killed by terrorist bombs and gunfire. Some have their husbands lying dead in a puddle of blood in the streets.

Tribulation is already in many regions of the world. In America we are seeing the horror of abortion. People simply don't want their babies so they put them to death. I want to shut my eyes as the news reports in our own America tell of mothers and dads who throw their children off of bridges, out of twenty-story buildings, take a gun and kill their children, throw infants into dumpsters, leave their babies sitting on the highway in boxes, lock them in cages and in basement dungeons for years, hold their heads under water in a bathtub until they drown, beat and starve them to death and the list goes on. There is no end of present day horrors that helpless babies and children face even now in this age we live in. This is why Jesus said the world would say, "Blessed are the wombs that are barren."

Signs of the end truly are everywhere we look. There is a noticeable shortage in physical things that are necessary for human survival on this earth. This too is a definite sign of a closing down world. I can look back and remember when the air was clean and fresh. Older folks can remember when we could draw water out of running streams and springs that never went dry, and there was no concern for polluted water. Now, our water supply around the world is filled with harmful elements and is unsafe to drink without extensive treatment. Today the air we breathe is filled with pollution and poison that is causing lung cancer and other respiratory illnesses. Nuclear bombs one day will poison what little air we have left. Today we have poisoned air, poisoned food and poisoned water. It's easy to say tribulation is at our doorstep.

These are signs upon the earth that we can notice and understand. We don't need some famous scientist to tell us hard times are ahead. Common sense tells us that our days parallel with what the perilous times the prophets said would come on the world. Even now our national leaders have realized there is no quick fix to world problems and many say now it could take years. The political promises are collapsing at their feet as our world increases its problems.

The collapsing economy will bring tribulation for lack of jobs and people will be in want. Our government cannot feed and pay the medical bills of all of America. Common sense tells us no jobs mean no money and no food.

When the pantry is empty and children are crying for food; that's tribulation. Jesus said, "Weep not for me, but weep for yourselves and your children. For the days come when they shall say blessed are the wombs that are barren and they say to the mountains, fall on us and to the hills, cover us." That's tribulation in the worst sense. When the world gets so bad that mothers fear to bring their babies into the world, it is tribulation. Jesus saw into the future horrible conditions.

Jerusalem: A Cup of Trembling

Jerusalem is the very nerve center of prophetical fulfillment in the word of God. Jesus said, "When you see these things come to pass, you will know that the time is near." One 'thing' He is referring to, when Jerusalem becomes a cup of trembling. Today Jerusalem is surrounded on every side with threatening forces and even now is at war with aggressors firing rockets into Israel. Tension is growing daily. Many of Jerusalem's surrounding nations are nuclear equipped to make a strike at any moment. Truly, Jerusalem is at this very moment a cup of trembling. God has said He would step in and defend Israel and all who move against her will be destroyed. When this happens, the end of the world will come.

Tribulation has already brought much suffering in the east and other parts of the world. Millions are starving and weeping in sorrow for the death of their children, and children are crying for the death of their parents. A lot of Christians are in denial about tribulation, they fail to see that even now we are having much in our world. We are seeing widespread fear and sorrow because of hate groups, evil men and terrorists and their growth around the world.

Training camps teaching young children to hate Israel and how to operate automatic weapons is active right this hour. These children are being brainwashed and controlled by evil men. Their path will leave behind them death, murder, and torture. They will have no conscience or mercy because evil has no conscience.

Those who help to destroy Christians and Jews are the devil's helpers. They are the devil's creations and he controls their minds to accomplish his evil plan. Christian parents teach their children to love everybody, but demon led forces teach their children to hate and murder. Even now little children are willing to strap bombs on their body and walk into busy market places and kill themselves and innocent, unsuspecting people. All of these events reveal a soon coming tribulation period that our world has never seen. As I previously said already we have much tribulation in the world. Lift up your heads your redemption draws neigh.

Population Explosion: Another Sign

Population explosion has caused China to pass laws that limit one child per family. It's hard to imagine growing up without a brother or sister, or nephews and nieces, but laws are being passed to slow down population increase. Even with these laws and millions of abortions, our world is still growing at an alarming rate. Mass population will bring even more suffering that no man can do anything about.

Many Americans are in denial of this fact as they walk through our well supplied Wal-Marts and giant food stores, and see fast food places on every corner in our cities. It would appear that we have enough food to last forever. However, if we had one worldwide drought our food store shelves would be empty in a short time. Tribulation will come to a nation of spoiled people who don't give God the time of day or thank Him for His blessings on America. We truly are a blessed nation, but it would never have been if it were not for the hand of the living God.

Let us each one give credit where credit is due, and even overdue. *To God be the glory great things He hath done.* Let us praise Him and thank Him every day of our lives, and pray for the millions who are starving and suffering all over our world. The day tribulation comes; we will understand what many others have been going through. None can feel the pain of others until they have felt the same pain themselves. This is why I believe Christians will be present during the great tribulation period. At that time our test of faith will reach its maximum test and only those that endure until the end will be spared.

When men do these things in a green tree how are they going to meet the trial of faith when the trees are barren, and the battle is fierce? There is a way, you know. It is the way of the cross. It is the acceptance of the blood and passion of Jesus Christ that make a way of escape from this present evil world. Jesus is the way, the only way. Fall down before Him. He is calling to all men to come and drink of the water of life.

Jesus doesn't want us to be miserable and unhappy. He wants the best for us. He wants to help us and love us. He is on our side. Trust in Him at all times; He is your friend. Signs of the times are in every direction I look. The prophets have spoken and what they have said will come in perfect order. Jesus said, "I came to seek and to save them that are lost, and to set at liberty them that are bound."

PART FOUR

PROOF
OF A
LIVING GOD

CHAPTER FOURTEEN
The Bible: Our Proof

IN OUR WORLD TODAY the very existence of God is questioned and denied, and our children and young adults are confused. Their faith in God has been badly weakened by television programs, and even the textbooks in schools. In this issue, I wish to reveal the truth about creation, and the proof that is revealed by the prophets in our Holy Bible.

The Bible records that have been in print for thousands of years, reveal many things and events that did not exist when our Bible was written. Only God has the ability to reveal future events which He did to the prophets long ago, and they have been written in our Bible by holy men of God.

Let us begin by the Genesis account of creation which has proven time and time again that a very intelligent mind designed and put our world and the planets in such a perfect order. We find that time and ageing has not changed this order which is necessary for human survival, and every living creature on the face of the earth. God gave us water, and soil to plant the seed for our food supply century after century which now feeds approximately seven billion people.

The seeds which are reproductive are necessary for life to continue as long as the earth remains. If seeds were not reproductive there would be no life, but we find that God placed everything there is from the minerals in the ground to the air we breathe for the survival of mankind. God knows the needs of mankind and He gives us every essential thing that we will ever need to live on this earth. As the Bible says, "Nothing that hath been made was made without Him." God made it all. The fact is, someone had to do it and only God has the ability and intelligence.

The Bible says, "In the beginning, God created the heavens and the Earth. The writers thousands of years ago wrote in our Bible the order of creation.

95

They told us of the animals that were lower in intelligence, and that man would have dominion over every living creature on the face of the earth. Man has proven this without question. I haven't noticed any apes flying a plane or doing surgery on one of their kind. They still haven't built a camp fire to keep warm, or planted a garden to have food. They still live in trees and don't have a hammer or nails to build a house for shelter. Not one of them has ever evolved into a human being. They still swing in the trees and screech with wild and undistinguished sounds.

The writers of our Bible have been dead for thousands of years, but time has proven their account is exactly right. How did they know the order of creation when books and libraries did not exist? I can answer that; God spoke through their minds as they wrote our Holy Bible. Many things were written in the Bible long before it happened. Therefore, someone had to have the ability to see into the future. Only God could possibly know and give out that information. That within itself is proof of the living God. May all who read this never question His blessed existence.

(Zechariah 14:12) *And this shall be the plague wherewith the Lord will smite all the people that have fought against Jerusalem. Their flesh shall consume away while they stand upon their feet, and their eyes shall consume away in their holes, and their tongue shall consume away in their mouth.*

These are the exact effects a nuclear bomb or missile to the human body. The prophet foretold this thousands of years before these inventions came into being. Our Bible is true.

(Isaiah 60:8) *Who are these that fly as a cloud and as doves to their window?* I believe the old prophet Isaiah saw a vision sent from God of a plane long before it was invented.

(Ezekiel 38:9) *Thou shall ascend and come like a storm, Thou shall be like a cloud to cover the land, thou, and all thy bands, and many people with thee.* This may speak of many planes coming for an attack to defend Israel and Gods children long before planes existed.

(Nahum 2:4) *The chariots shall rage in the streets, they shall jostle one against another in the broad ways: They shall seem like torches, they shall run like the lightning.*

This seems to be the automobile and possible satellites. We certainly can agree to the millions of accidents as people rush to get to their destination crashing together. The prophet saw into the future vehicles that he had never seen before and so he called them chariots.

In Luke 21:25, Jesus tells of the signs of the last days and the end of the world, He tells of the sea and the waves roaring, and men's' hearts failing them for fear, and for looking after those things which are coming on the earth. We today are seeing tidal waves and ocean turbulence beating at our coastal regions destroying homes and lives like never before in history. Truly the sea and the waves are roaring just like the Bible tells us. We can read the news of coming events right from the pages of God's Holy Word.

(Matthew 24:7) *And there shall be famines, and pestilences, and earthquakes in diverse places.* We have never in history witnessed as large of an increase in earthquakes as we are seeing today all over the world. In many world areas famine and hunger are already taking many lives. Insects are killing fruit trees and deer, and spreading many diseases. These things are truly visible this very hour and day. The Bible has never missed a mark as these events begin to unfold. This declares to all THE BIBLE IS TRUE!

(Matthew 24:24) *There shall arise false Christ's, and false prophet's, and shall show signs and wonders, Insomuch that if it were possible, they shall deceive the very elect.* Already we have seen many who have claimed to be Christ, and we have witnessed many false prophets who have deceived many and even led them to suicidal death. In Iraq this very hour, leaders are deceiving thousands by telling them they will receive great rewards in Heaven by blowing themselves up and killing innocent people. The Bible has foretold that these evil men would kill and deceive. I wish to encourage people to hold onto the word of God with both hands, and keep the word in their heart where no man can take it from you. By the word of God we find a lighted path that reaches all the way to glory.

(Amos 9:13) *The plowman shall overtake the reaper.* To me this reveals an age when our seasons will run together; they will be plowing at the same time of harvest. Simply, the seasons will have drastic changes. Global warming has already revealed a gradual warming trend and we are watching our giant ice caps melt and fall into the ocean. This will lead to drastic climate changes, and raging turbulent weather patterns such as severe hurricanes and tornadoes. Already we are seeing this change just as the Bible prophets have foretold. The Bible is true and God is real, for only he could reveal future events.

(Isaiah 30:26) *The light of the moon shall be as the light of the sun, and the light of the sun shall be sevenfold.* Today the sun's rays are causing skin cancer and we now have daily ozone alerts and warnings to wear sun screen when exposed to the sun. The sunlight which was always our friend has now become our enemy. The sunlight which was our blessing has now become our curse. Why? It is because of man's unbelief and refusal to obey the word of God.

Our experts say that global warming will result in catastrophic results in our weather patterns around the world. Tornado warnings rang out this past December of 2010 which is unheard of. We are having more tornadoes than ever recorded in history. Our weather patterns are falling right in place just like the experts predicted, and the Bible said would come on the earth.

The devil has tried to destroy the authenticity of the Bible. If he can accomplish this, men will live by their own rules and ignore God's holy word. Many today are doing just that. I believe that because men did not praise and thank God for all his blessings, He has lifted his hand of protection and care that all men will know that he is God and we are doomed without Him. God says in the Bible, "And they shall know that I am God." God gave revelation to all these events thousands of years before it came to pass. THE BIBLE IS TRUE!

(Romans 1: 28) *They did not like to retain God in their knowledge.* Just the other day a woman was kicked off a bus for reading her Bible out loud to her children. This past year the Governor of Georgia was criticized for suggesting that the people should pray for rain because of severe drought. To suggest the absence of prayer is to support unbelief in its strongest measure. They prayed and they got rain. God will honor all who pray and believe in his holy name.

Every direction I look, I see the very things that the prophets in our Bible have declared would come to pass and I've always believed that seeing is believing.

(Psalms 119:103-105) *How sweet are thy words unto my taste! Yea, sweeter than honey to my mouth! Through thy precepts I understand: Therefore I hate every false way. Thy word is a lamp unto my feet, and a light unto my path.* Believe the Bible for it is true. Jesus said, "My word is truth." My wish is to bring light to biblical events that no man can deny that will confirm the Bible as the absolute truth.

CHAPTER FIFTEEN
Creation

(Gen. 1:1) *In the beginning God created the heavens and the earth.*
(St. John 1:3) *All things were made by Him; and without Him was not anything made that was made.*

People all over the world are still searching for the origin of man. They study rocks, old bones, the planets and vegetation, and the search goes on century after century. This Christmas season atheists are complaining that they are being left out as Christians display all their nativity scenes and get much recognition in the advertising world, as they celebrate the birth of Christ. They sing songs that fill television and radio stations around the world, but I believe it's their own fault if they don't have anything to sing about. We Christians do and I for one will keep right on singing because I have something real to sing about. God is real, and I fear for all who deny His eternal existence.

Atheists are placing their slogans on buses, and placing signs in their yards and denouncing God by saying that there is no God. They say to stop worrying about it and live it up. They are right about one thing; they are going to be left out as the eastern sky splits and Jesus appears to take vengeance on all unbelievers and sinners, and takes His children to that eternal city where there will be pleasures forevermore without end. At that time all atheists will be cast into chains of darkness forever, and hell's torment will awaken their unbelieving hearts as they plunge downward into a bottomless pit of red amber walls of fire and heat. Their screams of pain will echo back off the walls only to remind them of how wrong they were. They now will believe one day too late. God has a better plan for all. He calls, pleads, waits and He gives opportunity today for men to repent and believe in His Holy name.

I found a letter to the editor in a newspaper which read, "Tracks were found in rocks which were said to have been made long before biblical history of man and creation. How do you answer to that?" How sad is it that people would believe Satan, who is a liar and a deceiver from the beginning. Tracks in rocks don't prove a thing because volcanic mud can be changed into rock in a short period of time. This is only the devil using the minds of men to blaspheme God and to promote unbelief in our world. The Bible is true and it says, "In the beginning GOD created the heavens and the earth."

Did you know that on the tallest mountain peaks they discovered marine life, and they say the only way it could have gotten there was if the earth had been covered by water at some time in history? If they would read their Bible they would find Noah's flood covered the whole earth including the mountains.

Have you noticed the many different kinds of animals in our world, each so perfectly designed? Have you ever noticed the many varieties of bird? There are so many shapes, sizes, colors, and each bird sings a sweet and different tune. How about the fish in the sea? There are a thousand different kinds, sizes, and colors with beautiful designs. Could all of these many creatures have just happened, or came into existence by themselves, or by an explosion somewhere out in space that became a living creature by some form of evolution? How ridiculous! Some animals live under water and die on land; some fly through the heavens and know when to go south for the winter.

Every creature has a brain, eyes to see, and a mouth to eat. The eye is a very complicated organ. It is able to take pictures and send them back to the brain, distinguish colors, and see obstacles that stand in our way. There can be only one creator of this. Only a master mind with extreme intelligent ability could design such a complicated body and perfect world, and that is God almighty creator and sustainer of the heavens and the earth.

How about a tree that draws sap in the spring? Trees grow leaves out of a tiny bud and provide apples, cherries, peaches, oranges, pears, plums, and a large variety of nuts that provides food for many creatures. Where did the wonderful fragrance come from that fills the air in spring when the honeysuckles and roses are in bloom? How can a single seed from a watermelon grow into a 50 lb. watermelon with hundreds of seeds inside for its future usage and growth?

All of these have such amazing features, flavors, colors, and sizes, but there is a more amazing fact yet. The human being was designed to enjoy all these foods, colors, and tastes. Not only do all of these remarkable things exist, but they provide the very substance needed for man's survival and health, and they fit our senses perfectly, with taste, vitamins, and minerals for human existence. So, immediately we discover that everything that was made was made for man's needs, and that each one fit perfectly to the five senses man was born with.

How ridiculous to even suggest that by a process of evolution all of these millions of plants, trees, and flowers so intentionally designed came into existence by their own power and design which was designed to provide for every living creature. I see clearly the hand and mind of God in every step of life I take. God is and will always be the only living force that has the knowledge and ability to design such a perfect order that has proved to meet the test of time and need.

Some insist that man came from a monkey by a process of evolution. This accusation is disqualified by fact. I am seventy-one years old and I have watched monkeys all my life and not one of them has ever passed their mile stone of time and evolved into a human being. This has never happened, not only in my lifetime, but going back thousands of years not one monkey ever evolved into a human being. If this did ever happen we would discover many humans walking around in our jungles without birth records. This has never happened nor will it ever because every living creature, tree, or flower was created by God alone. No human mind could put it all together in such perfect order as the perfect knowledge of the almighty God. He put it all together and it fits perfectly.

The ditches run into the creeks, and the creeks run into the rivers, and the rivers run into the oceans which are salt water, which purifies all the waters that run. Then the sun vaporizes the water which lifts into the clouds, rains upon the earth and runs once again into the oceans. God in his own wisdom built a perfect purifying system that has worked since the world began.

He alone is God and He makes all things perfect from a snowflake, to a drop of rain, to a leaf on a tree, to the freshness of spring, the heat of summer, and the chill of winter. He makes things perfect from the sprouting of a seed, to the harvest of grain, from the cry of a newborn baby, to a brain surgeon of vast knowledge and skill, from a child in the first grade to a designer of computers, and to surgeons who do heart transplants, and brain surgery. From children to men who build one hundred story buildings, and send men to other planets, no creature on earth even comes close to the abilities of mankind. Just like the Bible tells us, "God made man in his own image and after his likeness, and gave him dominion over the Earth and every living creature. It is in the intelligence of mankind where we see a small shadow of God.

The Planets Reveal God's Glory

When I was a small boy, I would look up into the sky on a clear night and see the big dipper, little dipper, and a million twinkling stars. Today, at seventy-one years old, I still look up on a clear night and behold the wonder of God's handy work, and I still see the big dipper, little dipper, moon and the millions of twinkling stars. After all these years time has not changed these spectacular formations that stay perfectly in their order that I saw as a child. Time simply has not rearranged the planets, they remain unmoved. A man cannot suspend a single feather in space for a second. I have tried it and it always flutters to the ground. God keeps an unquestionable order that baffles our scientists.

What would happen if the sun got to close to the earth? Answer: The earth would burn up. What if the sun were to get to far from the earth? Answer: The earth would turn to ice. If these conditions were to exist, our farmers could raise no crops. There would be no food or life on earth. The fact is though, the sun keeps its perfect distance from earth bringing to us spring, summer, fall, and winter century after century.

One might think with Earth rotating as it does century after century, it would spin into some distant galaxy so far from the sun that there would be no hope for its warmth and light, but it doesn't. We find that the planets have no chains or foundations to hold them in place and keep them in their perfect order as they are suspended in space to a degree that we can set our clocks, and measure twenty four hours in a day. Some power must control the universe and keep the planets in their perfect order to avoid total catastrophe. Truly the planets reveal the mighty hand of God holding the entire universe in his own hands. God is in control and He is never out of it.

(Job 28:9) *He overturns the mountains by the roots.* In Isaiah 24:20 the prophet says, "The earth shall reel to and fro like a drunkard." This appears to be saying that one day the mountains shall be moved out of their places, and the earth will lose its gravitational order. The only way this could possibly happen is that one day God would remove his hand that holds the earth and the universe in its order to let all men know that He is God and we are helpless without Him. As He has said, "And they shall know that I am God and there is no other God besides me."

(Genesis 1:1) In the beginning, God created the heavens and the Earth. This settles the question forever. Believe this because our Bible is true.

CHAPTER SIXTEEN
Creation: Part Two

EVER SINCE I WAS a very small boy the mysterious sounds in the night would catch my listening ear, and the millions of twinkling stars would stir my imagination. Where did it all come from, and how did it all get so perfectly arranged? After preaching the gospel and studying the Bible for these past thirty five years God has given me the answers that I did not know as a boy. In this chapter I will explain many points concerning God, man, and creation in my own words which I hope will bring light to all who read it.

The Bible tells us in Jeremiah 5:22, "Fear ye not me says the Lord: will ye not tremble at my presence, which have placed the sand for the bound of the sea by a perpetual decree, that it cannot pass it, and though the waves thereof toss themselves, yet can they not prevail; though they roar, yet can they not pass over it." I say to all God holds back the bound of the mighty ocean with the sand that he has placed there. He is God and there is none like Him. He opens the windows of heaven to send the rain, and replenishes the earth century after century so plant life can continue, and mankind can live and drink the waters of God's great and blessed resources.

God arranged the planets to move in such a gravitational order to control the seasons that we can enjoy spring, summer, fall, and winter. Without this perfect order human existence would be impossible to continue. The different seasons are necessary to continue in this perfect order to support our farmers, and our food and water chain. It's clear to me that this perfect order must be controlled by some force beyond the ability of mortal man. I'll say it without any hesitation; Only God has the power, the ability, and the wisdom to accomplish such a task.

God controls the universe and places every planet in a continuing order that is necessary for the earth to be productive for the needs of man. This just could not happen by itself because it would be impossible for the planets, the sun, and the moon to keep such a perfect order that we may set our clocks by the sunrise and the sunset. Twenty four hours in a day could not continue if the earth would speed up or slow down, but someone keeps the earth rotating at the same speed so that we can continue at twenty four hours in a day year after year. That somebody is the almighty God who made the heavens and the earth. Only God could ever accomplish such an impossible task, Only God could make all things right and perfect just as he has.

The Human Body Reveals Intelligent Design

The human body, to me, is one of the very best examples to reveal an intelligent designer with such wisdom to put together such a complicated being. The five senses that the human body enjoys are so complicated and so well designed that it would be impossible to grow by itself into such harmony that assist and supports this body, which promotes its very health and existence. Without the five senses the body would perish. God has given us not only life, but one surrounded by all of the things that help make our life pleasant and fulfilling.

(Psalms 139: 13-14) *God's word speaks of our body: For thou hast possessed my reins; thou hast covered me in my mother's womb; I will praise thee; for I am fearfully and wonderfully made.*

The human body is an amazing creation; let us discover its gifts and abilities. First of all, God gave us eyes to see and the eye is so complicated I'm not sure I can even describe it. Did you ever stop to think and notice how the eye was constructed? It sits back into the scull where it is protected from objects that could damage or destroy our vision. The eye is protected by an eyelid and eyelashes that blink in a split second to protect it from outside intrusions. That should be enough to convince anyone that a mind of great wisdom and intelligence constructed this human body. But, to describe the eye even further, it can take pictures of any object, send that picture to the brain and we see the image in its full color and beauty.

Although the eye is exquisite, what good would eyes be without something to see? God gave us the blue sky, and the fluffy white clouds. He gave us the white swan that floats silently across the blue waters of a lake. He gave us the ability to distinguish colors, and provided the endless beauty of the pink and purple sunsets, the rainbow, and a million varieties of beautiful flowers. With the eye I can see the beauty of a smile on a tiny baby's face, the falling snowflakes, and the harvest moon with a million twinkling stars. To suggest that the eye could form itself with such complicated features would be as ridicules as to say I could jump across the ocean.

When I walk through the woods and see a running creek, or when I hear the call of a crow as the sun rises on a fresh spring morning, I say in my heart, *Thank you God for your unspeakable gifts*. God sure knew what he was doing when he gave us so many things to see and enjoy. It's clear to see it was all given for man's good and pleasure. The whole universe was designed to fit and please mankind. It was God's plan to make us safe and happy.

Next, God gave us ears to hear with a tiny little eardrum that vibrates with the slightest sound and sends the sound to the brain that is able to distinguish what the sound is. The ear is able to tell us of danger or warnings. The ear can enjoy the sweet sound of music, hear a baby cry, or hear the distant thunder of an approaching storm. The ear can hear on a cell phone the voice of a distant loved one hundreds of miles away. It can distinguish angry, sweet or excited voices. The ear is equally as complicated to design as the eye. Say it with me; God sure knew what He was doing. Truly we are fearfully and wonderfully made with very intentional design. To God be the glory great things he hath done, and great are his creations.

God gave us the ability to feel; to know warmth or the cold, to embrace and to love, to feel the tender kiss of a small child, or the warm embrace of a friend or a loved one. The gift of feeling tells us of the sharpness of pain as a brier pricks our finger, or of the chill of winter that tells us to wear warm clothing. If there was no feeling in our body it would be self destructive. Sometimes our feelings are hurt, saddened or angered, and they cause us to smile or frown. They go deep into the soul.

God gave the body the ability to feel, to love, to hate, or to have compassion. He put together such a complicated body with so many abilities that no creature on earth can even come close to the mental capacity of the human being. To those who ask me where man came from, I can tell them in a hurry without question. God created the heavens and the earth and every living creature that lives and breathes. One day all will know that He is God.

The brain is another amazing creation by God. The brain is so complicated that I could never explain its fullest ability. The entire body would be useless without the brain. None of our senses would work without the brain. The brain has the ability to store in its memory bank for our lifetime, how to read, write, walk and talk, put sentences together or converse. Our brain has instinct that helps us to react in an instant to defend our body from harm or hurt.

The brain is creative and can build houses, automobiles, and computers. It is so creative it seems to be unlimited to new inventions day by day. The human brain has the capacity to learn new things as long as we live. Because of our brain, we can wiggle our toes and fingers, run at a faster pace, jump over a log, or swim across the lake. The brain is living proof of an intelligent designer that is able to connect it to operate every part of the body in perfect order. The whole body of man is connected with the brain and every single thing our body is able to do is controlled by it. Since it is very fragile, it is placed inside the skull where it can function without interruption or injury. Somebody sure knew what they were doing when they constructed man!

As I have explained the various parts of the body and how perfectly they have been designed to work in harmony with the whole body, we can see that evolution could never evolve anything into such a complicated and amazing creature. The human being had to be designed by a supernatural being capable of shaping any substance into any form he chooses. It was the God of creation, the only God who has all knowledge and wisdom. The only one who has no limits or boundaries to what He can do.

CHAPTER SEVENTEEN
The Big Explosion

SCIENTISTS HAVE MADE A theory that way back in the eons of time there was an explosion out in space and when the dust all settled there was the sun, moon, earth and all the planets. How ridiculous to even suggest that such an explosion could place all the planets in such a perfect order. Also, they claim that a static movement in the earth's crust formed a living cell and this cell eventually evolved into a living being which in process of time evolved into a human being. This creature first evolved into a monkey then gradually evolved into a human being. I've visited zoos all my life and they still look like monkeys to me. The monkey is just another one of God's creatures and their design is unchangeable, not by time or any other means. They will always remain monkeys!

Biblical record tells us that God made man in his own image and after His likeness. In view of that, man has a noticeable shadow of intelligence that stems from God that reaches beyond any other creature on the face of the earth, especially not from a monkey. Here is another absolute fact that man resembles the image of God in intelligence and abilities, just like God said it would be.

Man has intellectual abilities that single him out from all other creatures on the face of the earth, just like the Bible teaches. Fact is truth therefore the Holy Bible is true by fact. The monkey was not made in the image of God therefore it will never be anything else but one of God's creatures that God so perfectly created. This pattern will never be changed.

After a look at all the animals in the world, we find that each one from the giraffe with the long extending neck, to the lion whose roar rocks the jungle, and the elephant whose trunk carries heavy loads and is used to feed himself, reveals a very single design unlike any other creature. God made every living creature just as it pleased Him, and there is no two alike. I would run out of space to tell you about all the birds and the bees. But, each bird is so beautifully designed from the flamingo to the humming bird, and so different in its abilities and habits that any sensible person should clearly see that the many designs are far too numerous to just happen. Only an intelligent mind with supernatural abilities could shape and color such magnificent creatures.

Should we not give God credit for what he has done? Even the Indians who never opened a book in their life knew there was a higher power than man. I'll never understand why we that claim to be so well informed, and so educated stumble at the truth. Why do we accept theory when we have the facts in our Holy Bible? Why do we place the mind of God below the minds of men? Why do we search the universe for the origin of man and life when God has given us the birth record in clear detail of our first parents?

We have sent vehicles to other planets digging down into the surface and bringing that sample back to earth, then placing it under powerful microscopic labs searching for the slightest signs of life, but no life of any sort is ever found. I challenge anyone to take the tiniest speck of dirt from this green earth that God has so wonderfully created and you will find all kinds of life. There is only one planet that is fit for human existence in the entire universe and that is the earth that God so wonderfully and intelligently designed for life. We may venture out into space, but just like a boomerang we will always return to this green earth that God has places us on and given us to enjoy.

I've often wondered what God thinks as He looks down and sees the endless search of men looking for the origin of mankind, as they deny His eternal existence. One day God will say that they've searched long enough. He will have the last say to all questions as He appears in the eastern sky at the sound of the trumpet and every eye shall behold Him. My advice is to call upon Him while he is near, seek Him while He may be found. The day cometh when no man may be saved.

My prayer is that all who read this will have increased faith in the living God who truly created the heavens and the earth, and every living creature. It was God who sent his only son to die on the cross that every man could have opportunity to repent and be delivered from this present evil world. Hang the following scriptures on the door post of your home for all to see.

(Gen. 1: 1) *In the beginning, God created the heavens and the earth.*
(St. John 1: 3) *All things were made by Him and nothing that has been made was made without Him.*

CHAPTER EIGHTEEN
God's Perfect Order

EVERYTHING IN NATURE HAS a perfect order that fits into God's creation, revealing His divine touch. We see that a flower can never reach its peak of beauty and fragrance without the rain to refresh it, the sun to brighten it and warm it, and the clouds to cool it. This is comparatively true to the development of our spiritual stability. God develops every one of His children to a peak of fragrance and beauty by rainy days and clouded skies that are followed by the warmth of the sunshine.

Here is the secret of those we know who are so sweet and pleasant to be around. Their stability and fragrance was created by the great potter in whom they have placed their trust. The smile and the soft twinkle in their eyes that can be seen above the worn and wrinkled face only reveals the victories of overcoming that have callused them against the pain of defeat and failure. They have faced the hard places in life many times and have witnessed the joy as God's great hand led them on to greener pastures where the living waters flow.

We each one must stand on the lot where each battle occurs by our understanding and acceptance of the rainy days and cloudy skies that come for our stability and stronger faith in God. Someone once said, "We don't mind the hard road of trials when we know the road leads home." As God has carefully conditioned nature itself to progress and be healthy, so it is with our spiritual lives. God's whole armor was designed by himself to fit every Christian against every battle in life. The enemy's attacks cannot penetrate this armor. With it we stand and without it we fall. This armor is not made of steel and bolts but with the power and authority of the almighty God who can never be weakened or altered. His power is matchless and limitless. On the cross, He won all the battles that we will ever face. He knows our frame and he knows just exactly what we are in need of with perfect timing.

Acceptance of His salvation and Holiness given to us and earned on the cross is the only road to a victorious life. Without His holiness in our hearts, put there by His cleansing power by our request and acceptance by faith, the rainy days will worsen and the cloudy days will only get darker. Bitterness will daily rob your soul of God's joy and happiness. We must let God be God by giving Him the whole lump. He will shape and mold our lives, though sometimes rainy and cloudy until the fragrance and the beauty will be seen in the image and likeness of Jesus Christ.

Callused by trial only makes one tougher in trust, and brings victory over every battle. Sometimes we win, sometimes we lose, sometimes we laugh, sometimes we cry, sometimes we suffer, and sometimes we rest in sweet peace. But, understanding all of these conditions lifts us above the dark valleys because we know that all things work together for our good to those who love God. We know that if God be for us who can be against us, and greater is He that is in me than he that is in the world.

So come on rainy and cloudy days, for God is only conditioning me for the road ahead. God's perfect order works in the flowers of the field and it works in the sheep of His pasture. *For are ye not worth more than the grass of the field?* Only God knows just how to shape each one of us to accomplish His will. Never forget He is the potter and we are the clay.

CHAPTER NINTEEN
God Revealed

(Exodus 6:7) *And I will take you to me for a people, and I will be to you a god: and ye shall know that I am the Lord your God, which brings you out from under the burdens of the Egyptians.*

(Exodus 14:4) *That the Egyptians may know that I am the Lord.*

(Exodus 7:5) *And the Egyptians shall know that I am the Lord, when I stretch forth mine hand upon Egypt, and bring out the children of Israel from among them.*

(1st Samuel 17:45) Then *said David to the Philistine, thou comes to me with the sword, and with a spear, and with a shield: but I come to thee in the name of the Lord of hosts.*

The Egyptians found out the hard way that God is real as He sent the plagues upon them, and parted the waters as the children of Israel fled to safety. Their cries for help must have been heard as the waters closed upon their army. The Egyptians believed one minute too late as the waters covered their army that was in pursuit of the children of Israel.

It's no different today as Satan's army of unbelievers press God's children against the wall, trying to do away with prayer and their sacred trust in God. The battle continues as unbelievers fight against God to remove all evidence that would point to a living and true God. They hold to laws that Church and state must not mix and they fight against our leaders not to pray or mention the name of God. Just the past few weeks a ruling was introduced to stop promotion from the white house to declare a world day of prayer. If ever the world needed to join hands in prayer, it's today.

The absence of prayer in our schools has shown an increase in school shootings, violence, and a nationwide increase in teen suicide. This has caused parents to wring their hands in disbelief trying to find answers. To leave prayer out is to leave God out and at the same time support the atheist movement and let the devil in. The cold and lonely voices of our atheist promoters speak out as they search the nation looking for anything that would support a living God. Their hollow voices only reveal their empty hearts and their failing efforts. They are a minority group of God haters who grit their teeth at the sound of His glorious name. If they don't believe in a living God why does it upset them so at the sound of His name? Why would they fight against something that they believe doesn't exist?

As a minister of God, I wish to tell all the world of the results of a nation or of any individual who rebukes prayer or that doesn't pray. First of all, prayer to God is opening the fountain of all blessings, and when men cease to pray the fountain of blessing will be turned off. The reason men and women pray is because in this life we live there are many circumstances that are beyond human effort to solve. We know that God has the ability to solve those matters that we are totally helpless to do anything about. Only the devil would attempt to take away that hope that all of God's children have.

Secondly, prayer is the oxygen of life for all believers as they commune with God on their pillow at night. People give all their burdens to God each night and sweet rest comes as they sleep in peace. Of course, the devil works to rob us of our faith in God. He uses nonbelievers to work against God to cast a shadow of doubt against faith. These nonbelievers have been deceived by Satan and they are convinced of the lie that there is no God.

The word of God tells us in several places where men lost faith in God and turned to other Gods. At times like those, God sent His prophets to warn them of the action God would take unless they repented of their unbelief and turned back to Him. God sent word many times and said, "And they shall know that I am the Lord." That tells me that God has a limit and one day He will take action in such a manner that all unbelievers will know that He is real, and that He is in full control of this old world. In hell their screams of agony will reveal their grave mistake.

The Bible tells us that God will glean the earth of all the tares and the people who don't believe will be cast into the lake of fire along with Satan and his evil angels. Then, all unbelievers will know that He alone is God.

The God of love has given to us atonement for our sins when He sent Jesus to die on the cross that through Him we may have forgiveness of our sins. Jesus is our only salvation. Believing in Him we have hope of eternal life through repentance. God calls us to come boldly to the throne of His grace. This is the privilege of prayer that He has given the ability to let all requests be made known unto the Lord. He says, "Call and I will answer, ask and ye shall receive."

The greatest privilege we have on earth is the privilege of prayer, to talk to God on a personal basis, any time, and any place. He can give help at our time of need. The great apostle Paul said, "Pray without ceasing." It could very well be that Paul saw into the future a day that our legislators would sign documents to ban prayer in our schools and our world at a time when prayer is most needed. While they say cease to pray, Paul says the opposite.

It's no new attack by the devil where prayer is concerned. He attempted to stop Daniel from praying by ordering the people not to pray to the living God, but Daniel threw open his window for all to hear and he was thrown into a den of raging lions. Today as men order us not to pray we too should throw open our window so all will hear God's children praying. Our faith in God is revealed when we pray.

My mother told us children about a man who kneeled by his chair praying for his wife, and she was kicking him as he prayed to stop his prayers, but he kept right on praying. Unbelievers want us to stop praying, but we must keep on like the Apostles did when the place was shaken where they were assembled together. When men pray the prayer of faith, healing will come for the sick, and help will come for the lost. David said, "In my distress I called upon the Lord, and cried unto my God. He heard my voice out of His temple, and my cry came before Him, even into His ears."
(Psalms 18:6) *This poor man cried, and the Lord heard him, and saved him out of all his troubles. The Angel of the Lord encamps round about them that fear Him, and delivers them.*
(Psalms 34:6-7) *It is the wicked that refuse to pray, and it is the wicked who deny the eternal existence of God.* The bible says, "Many sorrows shall be to the wicked."
(Psalms 32:10) *One day soon God will stop all lying tongues who say there is no God.* Like the Egyptians who suffered many plagues for their unbelieving hearts, life ahead for all unbelievers is like a long dark tunnel where no light can be found. They walk on and on endlessly, but only to more darkness. They will eventually believe, but only in hell where demons mock and hiss at them as they run through eternity looking for a place of safety, and their screams only reveal their torment. They will then remember God's words, "And they shall know that I am God."

David, who was the most unlikely man in all the land to face the giant, was covered with armor from head to foot and all men feared him. However David wasted no time in declaring where his weapons lied. David yelled out for all to hear, "Thou comes to me with a sword, and with a spear, and with a shield, but I come to thee in the name of the Lord of hosts." David wound up his simple sling and the rock brought the mighty giant to the ground. When faith in God is real we become the victors and not the victim. It looked for certain that David would die by the hand of the mighty giant, but the stone that killed the mighty giant was soaked in the faith of the living God.

Sometimes our battles that we face look like the unconquerable giant, but when the God that we serve stands beside us we know that He will win the battle for His children every time. Nonbelievers face the giants with only the hand of flesh and they fail in every battle. It is foolish for any man to go into any battle without the whole armor of God snugly in place. To walk through the world without the whole armor of God is like walking naked through a valley filled with deadly snakes. No man can overcome the devil without the God of all power deeply embedded in his soul. All who don't believe in God must surely spend a lot of sleepless nights because the only real rest we can have is in Jesus who will never leave us nor forsake us.

I enjoy the quote, "When we pray, it is like pulling a rope that rings a bell in Heaven and God sends His mighty Angels to minister to our needs and rescue us from the pressing evils that are in the world." Like the song, *If Jesus Goes With Me, I'll God Anywhere*, real courage lies in our faith in God to help us fight our battles.

Faith in God can truly slay the giants and move the mighty mountains that loom before us on this earthly journey. Why would anyone deny the eternal existence of the living God when he has proven himself time and time again? God has opened the prison doors and set at liberty them that were bound by enemy chains. He has closed the mouth of lions, parted the waters, and quenched the heat of the fiery furnace. He is the master of the sea and the very joy of our soul. For one day, all men who are unbelievers in His eternal existence, God will take action. Paul calls them the enemies of the cross who fight against God, I believe God is a patient and loving God which He has proved over and over again, but He has a limit found in the scriptures.

When we pray we advance, we go forward facing the giants, and life's obstacles. By our silence we retreat and the devil wins the battle. A silent heart is a heart in need. Prayer on earth unites God's power with earthly crisis, and we plug in to the current of grace that is waiting in Heaven for us in our time of need. Let us get plugged in and lock it in for life.

CHAPTER TWENTY
The Tragedy of Unbelief

(Psalms 14:1) *The fool hath said in his heart, there is no God.*
(Genesis 1:1) *In the beginning God created the Heavens and the earth.*

In view of these scriptures I will continue the message to confirm the existence of the almighty God. Many live their lifestyle as if there is no God, church, prayer or morals. A Godless life is a life of sin. David said it best by calling one a "fool" who says there is no God.

In 1997, one hundred people went to their death at a rock and roll concert at a night club that caught fire and burned to the ground. The band used special effects such as fire and multicolored lights to excite the emotions of the dancers to wild and unnatural desires. It seems the wilder the scene the better they like it. I call it the dance of Satan because it leads to an anything goes attitude and opens the door to sin without guilt. However, this band's special effects were the cause of the fire that sent one hundred people to their death.

Common sense tells us we have went off the deep end and Satan has created a craving for wild and unruly events that drag our young people into a world of drugs, drink, and worldly pleasures. Sin and lust are at the top of the list that these gatherings promote.

A recent study revealed that the reason many young people don't attend church is because they don't believe in the Bible, which means they don't believe in God. Evolution now being taught in our school systems has turned the heads of our young people to the lie that there is no God. Suggestions about creation have put many question marks into the heads of our children. Where there is no God, sin holds no penalty or punishment. If you want to see a blood thirsty and evil world just convince our youth that there is no God. If you think our world is filled with crime and evil men now, just wait until the number of unbelievers increase in our land. This is why the Bible says, "In the last days evil men will wax worse and worse." Unbelief breeds evil and all the deeds of sin. If you don't take my word for it, just look out the window and you will see the fruits of unbelief.

I see a very sad and grim group of atheists standing around the graveside of their departed loved one as they believe they will never see them again. The absence of God at a funeral is the coldest and most empty atmosphere I can even imagine. God won't be in their midst because God doesn't walk with unbelievers who fight against the existence of God. Atheists, fight their battles alone. They face terminal illnesses alone, they face death alone and they face Satan and evil alone. The giants stand before them and they must face them alone. Demons invade their homes and families and enslave them to their unbelieving hearts.

Where there is no God, there is no moral responsibility, a conscience or guilt for sin. They have no need to repent because they believe there is no God. I wouldn't trust an atheist as far as I could throw my house. The atheist ambition is to destroy the name of Jesus and remove it from the face of the earth. They file petitions every day against the use of God's name publicly or in any other form. They want to remove anything that would suggest that there is a living God. Some stores have even changed the name of Christmas to Happy Holidays to support their cause.

I've noticed that atheists don't fight against Santa Claus, Rudolf the Red Nosed Reindeer, or Snow White and the Seven Dwarfs. They don't complain about a thousand other fictional characters. They don't say a word about aliens from mars or other planets. They will accept all of these, but put one sign on the town square that mentions God or Jesus Christ and they file a petition for removal. They will accept anything except the name of the true and living God.

They can't explain the amazing speed of a hummingbird, or the beauty of a million flowers that little birds dip their beaks into and sip dinner. They can't explain how a baby chick can live inside an egg shell without air to breathe. The list is long that atheists have no answers for and yet they insist to deny a divine creator who designed every living creature on the earth as it pleased Him. They can't explain how a tiny seed can grow into a large tree, and that one tree will have apples, another will have cherries, another will have oranges, another will have pears, or peaches. Then there are the trees that produce walnuts, pecans, hickory nuts, bananas, coconuts, which all are reproductive from generation to generation. I would like for them to explain all the many varieties and designs that grow around the world.

They can't explain how the first grain of corn, bean, or potato came into existence. It would be literally impossible for all of these food products to be self created, and to be the very things that would feed seven billion people in the world today not to count all the animals and birds. Each grain or seed had to have a beginning day for its life, and no seed can give life to itself because it has no mind. There is no way a seed could know it must grow in itself certain minerals that would flow through the blood stream of a human after it was eaten and digested. Only a mind of great wisdom could know all that was needed for the life of men. Only God has the ability to put life into a seed and make it grow and reproduce year after year. The biblical account of creation is the perfect answer to all our questions.

Everything that has been made is a perfect fit. No evolution process could even begin to accomplish such complicated and perfect arrangement. Look around you and see what God has done, look at the smile on a little girl's face. Look at the purple top clover fields and the tiny bees as they collect their honey, look up into the star lit night and see the handiwork of God. God has given us eyes to see, and ears to hear that we might know that He is God. Look up, for soon He will appear.

(Psalms 14:1) *The fool hath said in his heart, there is no God.*

God knew that one day men would say he doesn't exist. Unbelief is an evil word connected to Satan himself and many have been deceived by his lies. All who deny his existence are the devils helpers. The spirit of God is with me as I write these words and all who read this can only agree with me that He created the heavens and the earth. He is God and there is none like Him. I believe that the words I have written in this chapter prove without question the existence of a living God.

PART FIVE

OUR
CHRISTIAN FAITH

CHAPTER TWENTY ONE
What is Light?

(Isaiah 9:1) *The people that walked in darkness have seen a great light. They that dwell in the land of the shadow of death, upon them hath the light shined.*
(Isaiah 60:1) *Arise. Shine, for thy light is come, and the glory of the Lord is risen upon thee.*
(St. John 8:12) *Then spoke Jesus again unto them, saying, I am the light of the world; He that follows me shall not walk in darkness, but shall have the light of life.*
(St. John 3:20) *For everyone that does evil hates the light neither comes to the light, lest his deeds should be reproved.*

Jesus says I am the light of the world and in view of His words we must take a close look at what this light is all about. First of all in a spiritual sense, light is a revelation of truth, and also light is information given that all men might find their way from earth to Heaven. John said, "Behold thy light is come and truly Jesus is our light." He brought the light into a dark and lost world to guide our steps on the path of righteousness.

When Jesus came the world was filled with sin and darkness and today we find once again our world is getting even darker. Jesus gives us the reason in St. John 3:19, and this is the condemnation, that light is come into the world, and men loved darkness rather than light, because their deeds were evil. "For everyone that doeth evil hates the light, neither cometh to the light, lest his deeds should be reproved," this means they refused to give up their sinful ways.

Isaiah the prophet foretold of this very hour in our bible in Isaiah 59:9-10. "We wait for light, but behold obscurity; for brightness, but we walk in darkness. We grope for the wall like the blind, and we grope as if we had no eyes. We stumble at noon day as in the night." Noon day is the brightest time of the day which means that at a time when God had sent the true light in bright and brilliant beams by the Prophet's, by Jesus Christ, the mighty apostles, and many preachers of this day and age men, were ignorant as to salvation. There is only one reason and Jesus gives us the reason: Men loved darkness rather than light, which means they loved sin and worldly pleasures more than the light of God's truth. Because of this they stumbled in darkness in the brightest day the world has ever seen as if they had no eyes.

When Jesus came as the light of the world the whole world received spiritual light. The bible says, "He was standing in their midst and they knew Him not." It truly was the noon time of spiritual light, never had the world been lit up as it was the day Jesus came and walked the shores of Galilee. Truly, John got it right when he said, "Behold thy light is come."

The gospel of light has come in strong, plain language by spirit filled men of God, but men stumble in their lost and dangerous journey without God as they drink in all the sin the world has to offer, and cry for more.

What is Light

The light is God's spirit guiding us into all truth when we have accepted His spirit in salvation. God keeps a beacon of light ahead of us in our path on this earthly journey. This light is words given by the gospel of Jesus Christ and by the blessed word of God guiding our footsteps on the straight and narrow way. The way is narrow because Satan and sin crowd in from every side always pressing against God's children, always trying to darken the way before us. This is precisely why light is needed simply to see where we are going so we can stay on course.

God does not leave His children in the darkness, but gives us a well marked road map that leads all the way to glory. He makes the darkness light before us and gives us strength to make it over the steep hills ahead of us. David said, "His word is a lamp unto my feet and a light unto my path." God will not leave us in the dark but will make a way of escape from this present evil world.

This doesn't mean He picks us up and pushes us through the temptations of Satan, but it means He gives us light to make the right choices. God doesn't take away our ability to make choices, but He does give guidance to make the right ones. Every person that misses Heaven can only blame themselves for making their own choices and ignoring God's light that shines before every person to know the true way. What God says we must do, and the road He points out, we must travel. Doctrines of men and devils in our world today have turned men down the road to error and destruction.

God knew in His wisdom how wrong the minds of men will be when they think for themselves about the gospel and ignore the spirits calling to the way of Jesus. This is why the prophet said, "They blunder at noon time like blind men." God sends the light but too many walk in darkness. Jesus is the only way and there will never be any other way.

Today is the day of light, and opportunity stands before us, but soon God will turn out the lights forever in this world and obscure darkness will engulf the world forever. At that time all who preferred darkness will spend eternity in the blackest midnight that was ever known before throughout eternity.

A preacher I once heard on the radio said that many young people don't go to church because they don't believe the Bible. A mother was teaching a teen class and her daughter said, "I want to go to hell because that's where all my friends will be." Her mother wept as she told me the story. This young girl was resisting the light to salvation for earthly pleasures and associations with sinner friends. God alone gives light but in hell His light will not be found. It will be the loneliest atmosphere that ever existed as those who go there plunge downward in the bottomless pit and the sounds of laughter will be turned into terrible screams of agony which will pierce the black darkness forever and forever.

There will be no parties in hell, there will be no social life in hell and the fun time will be over. There will be weeping, wailing, and gnashing of teeth. The screams of agony will echo off of the red amber walls of the endless tunnels as the hot coals burn the feet of those who run through hell's flaming corridors trying to find a cool place to rest them. Hell is prepared for sinners and the ungodly and its burning flames can never be quenched or cooled.

Today God sends the light and He has done all He can do to rescue the perishing. He calls and calls and offers cool and living water for all. He offers eternal life in paradise where no pain will ever exist and all people will live in perfect harmony and peace in the heavenly presence of Jesus. It's sad so many trade a temporal life of sin for all of Heaven's glory and spend eternity in hell forever.

CHAPTER TWENTY TWO
Whom Shall I Send?

(Jeremiah 21:22) *I have not sent these prophets, yet they ran. I have not spoken to them, yet they prophesied. But if they had stood in my counsel, and had caused my people to hear my words, then they should have turned them from their evil way, and from the evil of their doings.*

(Jeremiah 1:7) *Whatsoever I command thee thou shall speak.*

(Matthew 10:27) *What I tell you in darkness, that speak ye in light: and what ye hear in the ear, that preach ye from the housetops.*

The prophets failed to say the words that God had told them to say, and they were speaking their own mind which led Israel down the wrong road to sin and evil. If men go into the ministry in order to have their say, or for the purpose of making a living, they have already left the spirit behind. When the minds of men replace the mind of God they have committed a great error. The bible says, "In the last days, men will become heady and high minded." This means an arrogant know-it-all attitude gives its own interpretations and ignores the Spirit's leading.

We must seek the mind of the Spirit and what the Spirit says in the ear, shout it from the housetops. If men would follow the spirit we would not have a thousand doctrines, many of which are false teachings, from the minds of men which in some cases are controlled by Satan. Paul made it clear what the doctrine was, when he preached Christ, and Him crucified. There is no other doctrine whereby men might be saved.

Like it was in Jeremiah's day, we have many who are failing to seek the mind of the Lord or to say the words that God commands them to speak. They even go so far as to say that God has told them things when again God has not. God will never change the doctrine of the Bible to fit a denominational privilege to engrave their doctrine. In the east they believe their doctrine is the right one ordered of God as they strap bombs on their bodies and murder innocent people. They have so set their faith in a false doctrine that they totally ignore the true God of love and peace. Here is where this scripture applies, "The wrath of man works not the righteousness of God.

Jesus Himself taught the one and only true doctrine that even a little child need not error therein. Only Jesus can provide salvation, and there is no other name under Heaven where men might be saved. Only Jesus was the Lamb without blemish. Only Jesus was qualified to die on the cross, the pure for the impure, and the innocent for the guilty. Jesus alone is the atonement for our sins and there is no salvation in any other.

When men, by omissions and additions, twist the scriptures to fit any doctrine on earth it will not change the words of Jesus who said, "Repent in the name of the father and the son and the Holy Ghost." We need men today who will preach the blessed truth, not for fame, or recognition, but because God has said, and we must obey. Who shall I send? Only those who preach the truth from the word of truth that are willing to stand in the gap for God.

CHAPTER TWENTY THREE
Be a Soul Winner

(Ephesians 4:11-14) *And He gave some, Apostles; and some, prophets; and some, evangelists; and some, pastors and teachers; for the perfecting of the saints, for the work of the ministry, for the edifying of the body of Christ: Till we all come in the unity of the faith, and of the knowledge of the fruit of the righteous is a tree of life; and he that wins souls is wise.*

There is a very good feeling about telling someone about Jesus every day, and when we do it makes the day seem so worthwhile. As Christians, we each have a burning passion to lead someone to Christ. It is never for our praise or our own glory that we desire to win a soul, but it is an inborn passion that comes naturally when one's whole self has been placed on the altar before God. When we say to God, "Here I am Lord, use me as thou wilt the passion of love for the lost will begin." The sweetest peace a Christian can have is when they lay their head on their pillow at night and know that they have told someone about Jesus and salvation.

As we move through the milestones of time, our world drifts farther and farther from God and salvation. God calls out to every Christian to win a soul. I believe the day is far spent, and the night is coming when no man can be saved.

My mother was a true soul winner for Jesus, and her heart was always searching for an opening to get a word in for the Lord. I've lay in my bed many nights as a very small boy and heard her praying for those she loved who were out in sin. Mother had a true burden for others who were lost and needed Jesus in their life. She always prayed aloud and it seemed like she was talking to someone right there in her bedroom and she certainly was. Always, at the end of her prayer, there was a peace that settled down in the darkness throughout the house and we children felt safe. I often found myself repeating mother's

126

prayers when the dark nights overwhelmed me. You might say mother tucked us in with her prayers every night.

One cold and rainy night, many years after we children had married and left home, mother told dad that she needed to go see an older man that was unsaved and talk to him about his soul. Dad reminded her that it was raining and cold and maybe they should go another night. Mom said no, and that God told her to go that very night. She told Dad that if he didn't take her she'd call their pastor to take her. Needless to say, Dad agreed to take her immediately. As they arrived they knocked on the door and the man opened it. Mother said without hesitation, "Buster, you are too good a man to go to hell, I want you to get saved." They kneeled with him at his couch and he gave his heart to the Lord. From that day until his death, Buster and his wife were in church every Sunday and joined in the work of the church.

One of the surest witnesses of the Spirit within is a strong desire to win a soul for Jesus, and one of the greatest blessings any Christian can have is to lead a person to Christ.

CHAPTER TWENTY FOUR
Forgotten Heritage

(Jeremiah 2:7) *And I brought you into a plentiful country, to eat the fruit thereof and the goodness thereof; but when ye entered ye defiled my land, and made mine heritage an abomination.*

It's a biblical fact that Israel turned away from God and drifted deeply into sin and idolatry which came after God had delivered them from Egyptian bondage and slavery. God had greatly blessed the land before them with rain from Heaven, but Jeremiah tells us they defiled the blessed land and turned the Godly heritage into evil abominations. This brought hard times ahead for Israel, and gives to us today an insight of what to expect if any nation does the same.

When I read this I get a picture of America which God has richly blessed over and over again, but like Israel, America has turned to many abominations and sin against God. Too soon America has forgotten where all blessings come from, and to give praise to God. Millions of Americans live as if God doesn't even exist, and their many sinful ways reveal God is no part of their life. Truly we are living in a day of forgotten heritage of our forefathers who founded America on the Holy principles of God.

No nation in the past that turned its back on God was ever blessed in their sins, but history reveals that disaster came to all who forgot the God of all blessings. Millions ask for God to bless America and at the same time live for the devil. The truth is, God will never bless those who commit wicked abominations before Him day and night. I shudder to think where America would be today if it were not for the praying churches all over. It is because of God's mercy and patience, and the prayers of God's children, that America still stands tall in the world in blessings.

Great shadows of famine are beginning to appear in our own America. A famine is something that comes on a nation because of the absence of God's protective hand of blessing. America will lose that blessing as she drifts farther and farther away from God and our Godly heritage. The Prophet said, "When the rains of blessings cease there will be the cry for wine in the streets," which means severe famine. Never forget, the seed that we sow will be the fruit that we bear in harvest, and those who sow iniquity will reap tears of sorrow, not only in this life, but in the life to come.

Terrorists all over the world have become an unstoppable force of evil that is dictated and controlled by the devil himself. Satan, who is supernatural, has the ability to control the minds of men and he dictates every evil act in the world, whether it be mass murder, when a man picks up an assault weapon and walks into an unsuspecting school room, or straps a bomb to their body and blows up all who are within range. Just this morning, five Americans were arrested for terrorist connections which tell us that we have very serious internal problems. September 11th, 2001 revealed an American citizen that Satan controlled and used like a mechanical Robot to destroy innocent lives.

Many streets in America are now unsafe to walk on or even drive a car on because of evil Americans who have forgotten their Godly heritage. There are even bust tours available to the public that will drive through these evil streets to view the evils that can be seen through the windows of the bus. This means that people actually pay a fee to see the evils that exist on our own American streets all over America.

Sex perverts prowl our neighborhoods and abduct our children and use them in horrible and unthinkable sex acts. Our own American citizens take little children and brutalize and murder their own children. Crime scenes are the act of the day in broad daylight in peaceful neighborhoods. The moral condition of Americans today reveals a carefree and heartless generation that commits sin without moral embarrassment or guilt. The gay populaces walk our streets hand in hand and demonstrate for gay marriage rights while our children look on and wonder why people get so mixed up about marriage and family life.

Many Americans have become lazy and irresponsible people who only care about themselves, so they rob and murder good responsible people to feed their demonic controlled minds. Today we are seeing a sin malignant society that has forgotten there is a God to answer to for their sinful and evil ways. When we look about us, the view is so depressing that many just turn their heads trying to find a better view, but unfortunately, every direction we may look, we only see more of the same.

No generation in the history of man has ever been so morally corrupt as this generation. The wild craving of our young people for parties, drugs, and sex, have taken away all desires to protect their reputation or their Godly heritage. Many could care less about the millions who have given their lives on the battlefields to protect a Godly heritage, and the American way of life. It makes my heart sad as I stand by helplessly unable to turn men to God, and the decent way of life. What so many have died for should be protected by every American, and unless we each one do our part we will see the death of a great nation.

Jeremiah reminds us of God's blessings He has given us for life and prosperity, and Jeremiah also warns us of the results of turning away from God. Only God can heal the wounds Satan has inflicted on our nation to destroy it, and God will only heal our nation if America gets on her knees and repents of her sins and turns back to God. When we leave God out, the devil moves in and evil takes rule. Let us turn to Jesus who died for our sins and has power to heal our land.

Trust is more than just a word, it's an action that comes from deep within the heart that connects to God's power and grace by our own faith. If the connection is not working, it's because trust is not elevated to the height as it should be. Trust and faith plugs in to the current of God's Grace.

CHAPTER TWENTY FIVE
In View of the Old School

(2nd Timothy 3:1-8) *Know this also, that in the last days perilous times shall come. For men shall be lovers of their own selves, covetous, boasters, proud, blasphemers, disobedient to parents, unthankful, unholy, without natural affections, trucebreakers, false accusers, incontinent, fierce, despisers of those that are good, traitors, heady, high-minded, lovers of pleasures more than lovers of God. Having a form of godliness, but denying the power thereof from such turn away, for of this sort are they which creep into houses, and lead captive silly women laden with sins, led away with divers lusts, ever learning, and never able to come to the knowledge of the truth. Now as Jannes and Jambres withstood Moses, so do these also resist the truth: men of corrupt minds reprobate concerning the faith.*

The Bible gives us the world's condition from the results of loose living and ignoring the godly instruction of the older folks who many say are just victims from the old school. To me that is like saying we are out dated and behind in knowledge, and wisdom. In this message I wish to revisit the paths of the past and defend those of faith who have witnessed all the obstacles in this path of life that they have overcome many times over.

I believe that the learning schools of life are not expanded by divorcing the wisdom of those we often say are from the old school or maybe are 'old fashioned' and out of touch with reality. I will say it without hesitation; the better parts of my life are the parts that I was taught from my grandparents and my parents. They were from the old school that taught family values, and what it means to live a righteous life in an unrighteous world.

Our modern electronic world that is filled with computers and new inventions everyday leaves behind many of our elderly folks from the old school. They stumble at all the new technologies. Many of our old folks stand aside feeling lost in a fast moving world and find it very hard to catch up or to stay in step with this new generation of electronic minded people.

These old folks from the old school may be electronically stupid, but they have knowledge and wisdom that can't be found in the storage banks of the computer world. For the most part, our old folks are ignored and are said to be outdated by modernism, and most are taken lightly when it comes to advice. I heard a young college student telling her mother, "These old folks have no idea what is going on in our world." I thought to myself, how wrong and short sighted this young woman really was. It was here that a picture came before me as my memory went back in time and I found a treasure chest of wisdom from those old folks from the old school.

I found in my life the seeds of wisdom that had been planted by my grandparents and my parents that still bears fruit today. I also found that the things that really count in life came from the wisdom of the past. I don't believe that wisdom is confined to the past, but when it is left behind the future will be barren and suffer greatly. So let us include the old school along with the new school by recording the wisdom of the past along with the wisdom of the future because no wisdom should ever be forgotten or ignored.

One day, my mother was in the garden with my grandfather picking cucumbers and every once in a while he would find one that was too big. He would pitch them over the fence in the weeds. Mother asked him why he threw the oversized ones in the weeds. Grandfather answered by saying he would rather throw them in the weeds than take them to the house and hear maw gripe because he had allowed them to get too big.

I call my grandfather a real peace maker by his act that day in the garden. Grandfather hardly ever complained about anything in front of his children or his wife. He just accepted things as they came. The cucumbers were only one of many seeds of family values that grandfather taught his children over the years. All the computers in the world could not replace that.

I'm thankful that I had Christian parents who taught me family values that were seasoned with biblical instruction. I was taught responsibility, and how to be a responsible person to those around me. I was taught the importance of our family reputation in our community. It was very important to those of the past what your neighbors thought of you. We were taught to be respectful and considerate of others who had less than we did, and even share with those who were in need.

I remember my dad driving several miles to pay back a few cents that someone had overpaid him at the store. Honesty was programmed into our minds by the honorable acts we saw in our parents. Dad only had a fourth grade education, but he held a treasure of wisdom brought down from his father and mother about life, about love, and most of all, about God.

Today many things that really matter are left behind such as God and salvation, about reputation, and responsibility, as our children run the way of the world. Today they plan their week for fun, and play, and give little thought of what the neighbors might think about their family reputation. Little thought is given when the news reports our neighbor was arrested for drugs or drunk driving. It just seems to be expected in this world of forgotten values from the old school.

Real wisdom is not how much you know about the electronic world, but it is knowing family values and practicing them every day. Unbending values is what makes an honorable family, and an honorable nation. When we take lightly the advice and leadership of our older generation, we need to stop and think. They have faced every issue we will ever face many times over. When those that are young walk a new path in life we must remember that grandpa and grandma have already walked and conquered that very path many times over and their advice should be treasured and respected.

When men ignore the spiritual wisdom of the past they will promote a permissive spirit whose origin is from the minds of men. Spiritual wisdom is learning something from God that supports the will of God by biblical instruction. Those older folks who hold fast to the things God has taught them should not be taken lightly because God is the oldest school of all, and He will be right every time without room for change.

When I hear an older person talking about the good old days, and see the sparkle in their eyes, it tells me they are glad that they were a part of them. The changes that have engulfed them only make them wish that men would live in harmony with the values that they respected and lived by.

I'm not against change in a materialistic sense, but I am against change in a biblical sense. For instance, if I were stranded in the wilderness with another person in zero degree weather and I had matches in my pocket to start a fire, and he begin to rub two sticks together to start his fire, I wouldn't get me two sticks and begin rubbing them together. I would simply reach in my pocket, get out a match and strike it for my fire. Thank God for matches, and thank God for many other changes that have greatly improved the struggles of life. However we must define two different kinds of change that must not be overlooked or avoided.

Spiritual change is quite different than that of a material change because spiritual change from the Bible must never happen. We must continue telling the old, old, story of Jesus and His love, and the gift He gave to all who would believe in His name. We must always accept the teaching of the Bible about sin and forgiveness that was provided on Calvary.

The Bible gives us instruction on what sin is in vivid detail. Sin must never be covered over by a modern and selfish generation that ignores what the Bible teaches and decide things for themselves. We must never change the rules of righteousness that God has inscribed forever in His word. What sin was in Noah's day, and the days of Lot when God rained fire and brimstone on Sodom and Gomorrah thousands of years ago, is still sin today. God will never change His mind about sin and righteousness.

God's word is established forever and woe unto those who attempt to change it. When we stand before God to be judged on judgment day we will not be judged by what we think, but each one will be by the blueprints of righteousness recorded in the holy word of God. The Bible says, "Heaven and earth may pass away but my words will never pass away."

I believe the older generation holds more closely to the word of truth, and with each passing generation it is clearly visible a continuous drifting deeper and deeper into worldly actions and acceptance by our younger generation. Our leaders say we have to accept change or the church will die. I feel it depends on what things we change that will make a difference. For instance, indoor plumbing is fine, but indoor worldliness is sin, and we must not shape the church to fit the world, but we must shape the church to follow the steps of Jesus and His word. I still believe in old time religion that came from the word of God and was carried on by the old school of the past that finds men that are lost and imprisoned by Satan and sets them free.

Our scripture says, "Ever learning, and never able to come to the knowledge of the truth." It seems we know a lot about everything on earth, but very little about God and truth. Many fail to know how to live righteously before God and before man because their desires have stored worldly wants. Their wisdom then is not from God but by self made choices. If our younger generation, and older as well, would wish to learn about God as strongly as they do about texting, and computer knowledge, I wonder what kind of changes America would witness.

Today in our own America we have those who wish to remove our flag from public display that stands for justice and liberty for all men. Our flag also symbolizes those who have fought and died for these very causes. Our flag is not an idol, as some would say, but everywhere it is lifted and waves in the wind it calls out to our fallen dead and gives honor to their ultimate sacrifice. Those who enjoy the liberty we have in America sleep in peace at night in luxurious beds and shop in our countless giant stores of abundance, but at the same time denounce our flag that waves to the world with a voice that says liberty and peace for all.

These people need to be sent to some distant planet that matches their own barren minds. They have forgotten about the millions who have spilled their blood around the world so we could have a place of safety, and equal opportunity to learn and prosper. These flag haters have forgotten about evil dictators sent from the devil himself who take away our freedom and drive us around like herds of cattle. Were it not for America the whole world would be in chains, and misery would be the order of the day. I shudder in my soul to think how it could be were it not for our own America, and those of the past who held on to the plows of righteousness.

Yes, I'm from the old school, and I'm proud of it. I still sing our national anthem with respect and pride. I still pray at night before I close my eyes in sleep to the God of the high heavens who sends His angels to maintain our safety, and our peace. My eyes are set on Jesus because I know He is our peace, and our only salvation. My ears are open to those from the good old days whose faces are wrinkled with age because I know they have already been through the battles I must face ahead of me, and they know the spiritual artillery that works.

I will listen because I know they possess wisdom by experience of trials and hardship. I will listen because their faith in God is revealed by the values they never bend, and I will follow in their steps. I will listen because their words are backed up by their success. I will listen because truth and God is the foundation of their home and life they live.

If America ever returns to the values that our forefathers founded, America will have to go back to the old school where Godly values began and take hold of them once again. Read the scriptures at the beginning once again and think of the present condition of America and the world as you read them. You will see a picture of a world that has forgotten values taught in the old school that parallel with this very day of evil and violence. We can do better.

Poor responses to truth and wisdom bring bad results in men's life.

CHAPTER TWENTY SIX
The End of Our Journey

THE CHRISTIAN LIFE HAS a beginning journey where we begin our long and often weary journey. Our journey began when we fell on our knees before God, repented of our sins, and invited Jesus to come into our hearts. The first miles of our journey were the growing and learning days which were exciting and joyous as we met new friends and found our place in the church serving God. However, we soon found that the way often had valleys to cross, and mountains to climb. There were battles to be fought and impossible situations to face. Sometimes the way became lonely, and we felt alone as we visited with family and friends who were living in sin. We could not join in their games or walk in their ways as they traveled the broad way that led to destruction. When you walk with Jesus it's a different path, and a different journey, but it's a blessed journey and I wouldn't take anything else for my journey now.

(Eph. 2:1-5) *And you hath He quickened, who were dead in trespasses and sins; wherein in times past ye walked according to the course of this world, according to the prince of the power of the air, the spirit that now worked in the children of disobedience, among who also we all had our conversation in times past in the lusts of the flesh, fulfilling the desires of the flesh and of the mind; and were by nature the children of wrath, even as others. But God, who is rich in mercy, for His great love wherewith He loved us, even when we were dead in sins, hath quickened us together with Christ.*

(Ephesians 2: 19) *Now ye are with the saints and the household of God.*

The Christian walks a righteous path with Jesus and can no longer walk where they once did in times past and in sin. Now the journey traveled is quite different. Most importantly, you don't walk alone even though it may seem so because Jesus walks with you giving strength, and guidance. His still, small voice comforts the soul often on your journey and your strength is renewed.

The beginning journey has an ending and a destination. Heaven awaits all who faithfully follow Jesus and walk in His ways.

I can visualize even now a weary and tired Christian who has fought and won the battles against the tempter, who has faced the storms of life, and the scars and hurts that often burden the journey. They come to the river Jordon, their journey has been long and tiring with many battles and persecutions that Satan set in their way. Now they stand on the banks of Jordan, the river is raging, the waves are high, and they have traveled the last mile of their journey which most often is the hardest mile of life. Now as they stand on the banks of Jordon they can see the brightness of Heaven glow across the river. Home is in sight, but one last battle stands before them. They must cross the river to where the city of God lies. The winds are blowing, the river is raging. They trudge on and refuse to turn back because now at last they have the city in sight.

As their feet touch the stormy waters a form appears before them His hand is reaching out to them and they grasp hold. It is the hand of Jesus there to lead them on into glory. Their mind goes back to that old song, *I won't have to cross Jordan alone, Jesus died all my sins to atone, through the darkness I see, He'll be waiting for me, and I won't have to cross Jordan alone.* Jesus will be there to guide us safely across where the atmosphere will take our breath away. It will be worth it all when we see Jesus. Just one glimpse of His dear face, all sorrow will erase. It will be worth it all when we see Christ.

The end of the journey in this life will come to all, and as we stand at the river's edge of eternity may our chin be up in true faith as we walk the last mile of the way. Mine and my wife's journey that I have written about, that began in the mountains of Kentucky, has reminded me once again that we all have our mountains to climb and our valleys to cross, but there is always a hand to hold to and to lead us on to victory. The hand of Jesus has a sure grip that will hold on when we are too weak and our strength is almost gone. He is our Savior and our redeemer. Trust in him at all times.

Today Fran and I are retired but the flame that God started burning in our hearts is still burning today and we both have no regrets, only praise for this journey He has led us in. We have found in Him a true friend. We both are in good health and if you are looking for us on Sunday you'll find us in church praising our Lord and feasting on manna.

Earthly blessings are only a tiny taste of what Heaven holds for the children of God. There are treasures waiting in Heaven for all of God's faithful followers, and Jesus will have the table spread with delights that will outshine and replace all our longings for the good old days that we will leave behind forever.